To Nina Bawden, another superb writer,
with admiration and love

About the author

Nicholas Tucker was first a teacher and then an educational psychologist before becoming Senior Lecturer in Cultural and Community Studies at the University of Sussex. A frequent reviewer and broadcaster, he has written many books on children and reading, including all three volumes of *The Rough Guide to Children's Books*, the final one with Julia Eccleshare.

Acknowledgements

I would like to thank Philip Pullman for his generous help, which made writing this book so much easier as well as more satisfying. Also a big thank you to Geoff Fox and Kim Reynolds, for their unfailing and always stimulating interest and support. Kate Agnew was a marvellous editor, coming up with a whole series of excellent suggestions, and Simon Flynn set the highest standard for co-operation as my publisher. Students I have taught at Sussex University and at the Roehampton Institute have also helped me greatly over the years, as have my own children and now grandchildren in all matters to do with children's literature.

Darkness Visible

Inside the World of
Philip Pullman

NICHOLAS TUCKER

Published in the UK in 2003 by Wizard Books,
an imprint of Icon Books Ltd., Grange Road, Duxford,
Cambridge CB2 4QF. Tel. 01763 208008. Fax. 01763 208080
e-mail: wizard@iconbooks.co.uk
www.iconbooks.co.uk/wizard

Sold in the UK, Europe, South Africa and Asia by
Faber and Faber Ltd., 3 Queen Square, London WC1N 3AU
or their agents

Distributed in the UK, Europe, South Africa and Asia by TBS Ltd.,
Frating Distribution Centre, Colchester Road, Frating Green,
Colchester CO7 7DW

This edition published in Australia in 2003 by Allen & Unwin Pty.
Ltd., PO Box 8500, 83 Alexander Street, Crows Nest, NSW 2065

ISBN 1 84046 482 8

Printed and bound in the UK
by Clays of Bungay

Contents

CONTENTS

Illustrations

ILLUSTRATIONS

Philip Pullman

Philip Pullman

Philip Pullman was born in Norwich in 1946, the son of an RAF fighter pilot. Moving around from station to station with his younger brother Francis, they settled for a time in what was then Southern Rhodesia. Returning to Britain, they heard that their father had died in a plane crash during a raid made against the rebel Mau Mau movement in Kenya. Neither son knew their father at all well, since he was so often away from home. He was awarded the Distinguished Flying Cross after his death, and there are newspaper pictures of Philip, then aged seven, standing outside Buckingham Palace with Francis just after his mother had received the medal on behalf of her late husband.

Years later, while going through some family papers, Pullman discovered that his mother and father were planning to divorce at the time of his father's death. This was a considerable shock, given that any hint of this family secret had previously been

FROM DRAYTON TO THE PALACE

TWO Drayton boys—Francis and Philip Pullman, aged five and eight—went with their mother, Mrs. Audrey Pullman, to Bucking ham Palace yesterday The picture shows them after Mrs. Pull man had received from the Queen the Distin guished Flying Cross conferred on her hus band, the late Flight Lieut. Alfred Pullman R.A.F., for gallantry in operations against the Mau Mau in Kenya Aged 38, he was killed in February.

Mrs. Pullman was re ceived by the Queen in a private room at the Palace. Afterwards Mrs Pullman said: " The Queen shook hands with both my boys and asked me how long my husband had been in the Air Force, and how old my sons were."

Mrs. Pullman said her husband's D.F.C was the first medal awarded during the Kenya operations.

'Huma when h recorde

" Human falli official statement for a baby girl Hospital, Maccles recorded as a bo
The mother M Wilmslow (Ches was told, "It's a round from the child was later Jeffrey James.
After an investi today, the secreta and District H Committee issued ment:—
" We are quite is no possible the babies. births in the one at 7.20 in and the other 5.15 in the even
" That also wa fortunately, thro on the part of wife, was recor
A report of the sent to the Mini Mrs. Cooper o when she foun and not a boy

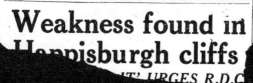

Weakness found in Happisburgh cliffs

'T' URGES R.D.C

1. Article from the *Eastern Evening News*, 3 November 1954. (Reprinted courtesy of the *Eastern Evening News*, Norwich.)

kept from him. But even without such knowledge, which came to him late in his career as a novelist, it is not surprising that Pullman often creates young characters in his fiction who have problems with their parents, sometimes stretching far back into the past. Dead or missing fathers are also a constant occurrence in his stories, and Pullman himself remembers that he was 'preoccupied for a long time by the mystery of what [his father] must have been like.' That mystery continues to the present day, in the sense that Pullman still feels certain that there was something not right about the reasons given for his father's fatal accident. But his efforts to find out more have so far proved unsuccessful.

Returning to Britain, the two boys stayed in a Norfolk rectory with their mother's parents while she worked full time in London. Pullman's grandfather was an Anglican clergyman, who used to tell the boys a range of stories from sources that included the Bible as well as tales he had heard in his role as occasional prison chaplain at Norwich Gaol. One of his grandfather's jobs was to accompany prisoners to the gallows after they had been condemned to death. With money always tight, he took up this additional duty as a matter of course. The boys were never aware of any extra strain, since their grandfather would not have wished to upset them about this part of his life or indeed about anything else. It was only years later, when Pullman was an adult, that his grand-father told him of the pain that this part of his job had caused him.

Far from turning him against religion, Pullman now remembers his grandfather as 'a wonderful man: gentle and humane as well as being a marvellous storyteller.' He has also described him as 'the most important influence in my life.' Very much a tradi-tional head of the household, and a gratifyingly important figure in the village, the boys' grandfather could be playful too. Above all, he was a man 'in whose presence you *wanted* to be good.' Pullman still loves the traditional language and atmospheric settings of the Bible and the Book of Common Prayer, so associ-ated in his own mind with his grandfather. There were also regular visits to church and Sunday School during these years. Pullman makes use of Biblical stories and imagery throughout *His Dark Materials*, even though his feelings have now turned against the Christian religion that he no longer believes in.

There was never enough room in his mother's small London flat for her children, nor could she afford to give up full-time work. But a child's fantasies are not concerned with objective reality. So it's also possible that some of the hostility felt for that ambiguous mother Mrs Coulter in *His Dark Materials* dates back to the small boy's anger and bewilderment at having been, in his eyes, temporarily abandoned by

2. Philip on right, aged about seven. (Reproduced by kind permission of Philip Pullman.)

his own mother. Mrs Coulter, after all, combines both strongly positive and utterly negative images of womanhood. Could this contradictory mixture also reflect some of the conflicting feelings Philip may occasionally have felt towards his mother at the time? Now no longer alive, does she continue to live on in a number of her son's best works?

Pullman has, however, stated that Mrs Coulter is easily his favourite character after her daughter Lyra. Beautiful, wicked, unpredictable and amoral, her presence is always exciting. Absent mothers often attract all sorts of fantasies in the imagination of the children they leave behind, not all of them by any means negative. Mrs Coulter's undeniable charm and feminine allure, for example, are at one with the fantasies the young Philip had about his mother's supposedly fast-paced and glamorous city life away from her country-based family. Visiting her in London he remembers admiring her general sense of style so different from the simplicities of rural Norfolk. There were also exciting theatre visits, and encounters with her various hard-drinking friends.

As for any feelings of resentment he may once have had, in conversation now he insists that at the time he took her absence for granted. He believes there was never any suffering on his part simply because his grandparents were providing all the love he and his brother needed. Living in a large rectory, the boys had plenty of room to play, constantly diving into their grandfather's extensive dressing-up collection, so often put to use in the various village pageants and processions he liked to organise. There was also a large garden and the run of the village at a time when traffic was minimal.

His equally loving grandmother is also remembered by Philip as constantly warm and gracious, as well as sharply intelligent. Her sister lived in the household too, a maiden lady who had been disappointed in love and had since become, in Pullman's own words, 'a bit of a drudge.' Somewhat frail and also totally devoted to the boys in a way that Pullman has described as simple-hearted in the purest sense, she made up the trio of older adults who provided the two children with an atmosphere of unconditional love.

Aged eight, Pullman attended a prep school near Norwich. It was there that a kindly teacher once read him and fourteen other boys the whole of Coleridge's famous poem *The Rime of the Ancient Mariner*. Listening spellbound, Pullman felt gripped as never before, and began to wonder about one day becoming a writer himself. By now a stepfather had come along, also an RAF pilot, and the new family travelled halfway round the world in an ocean liner to a posting in Australia. In time Pullman was also to make long boat journeys to the Suez Canal, Bombay, Aden,

3. A school photo of Philip at eight years. (Reproduced by kind permission of Philip Pullman.)

Colombo, Las Palmas and Madeira as part of the restless life of any child whose father or stepfather was in one of the armed services.

It was on this particular voyage to Australia that the two boys, when both came down with scarlet fever, started inventing games as fierce as they were intense. Using a plastic construction kit to build forts and castles, they played out various imaginary conflicts for days at a time, each boy taking the part of either the good or bad guy as the situation demanded. Once they were settled into their new home, such games then became influenced by the Batman-style comics, which the nine-years-old Philip totally adored.

There was also Australian radio, with its serials about Superman, cowboys and a kangaroo that kept tools in its pouch. With these this remarkable animal could repair almost anything, including broken-down trains, so saving valuable lives. Pullman now believes that it was the adventures of this kangaroo that actually started his career as a storyteller. Each night, when the boys had gone to bed in their shared room and the light was turned off, Philip would sing out his version of the heroic kangaroo's radio signature tune. There would then follow a story made up on the spot, with neither Philip nor his brother having any idea how it would end. Pullman can still recall the feeling of excitement as each story seemed to find its own particular path, just as his stories do today, often to the surprise of the author himself. That section of the National Curriculum that requires all pupils in schools today to make a plan before writing their own story is particularly detested by Pullman. For him, this is the equivalent to killing off the imagination before it has even had a chance to get started.

The following year Philip, now aged ten, was back in Britain, first at a prep school in Battersea and then at Ysgol Ardudwy, a state school in Harlech: the last of the eight different schools he was to attend. This coincided with a move by the whole family to Wales, with Pullman's stepfather resigning as an RAF pilot to concentrate instead on civilian flying. He was now also acting as a father for four children, two more having been born after he and Pullman's mother had married. The part of North Wales they chose to live in was to provide Pullman with what he now remembers as 'a wonderful time':

> We lived up in the woods, about a mile above [a] very small village, right at the edge of a hill. We just wandered all over the place, there were no boundaries … It was a time when children were allowed to and indeed expected, really, to leave the house after breakfast and not come back till darkness fell. And many times we did that. So I had a sort of wild and very unsupervised time, which was just great.

At school while his brother was making model aero-planes and volunteering for the Air Training Corps, Pullman preferred to spend his spare time reading, writing poetry, painting or strumming on his guitar. But from the age of thirteen he also came under the influence of an inspired English teacher named Enid Jones, to whom he still sends copies of his latest books. Her unfailing support and enthusiasm were impor-tant factors in helping Pullman to win a scholarship in 1965 after taking the entrance exams for Exeter College, Oxford, in order to study English. He was the first pupil from his school ever to go to Oxford University; winning a much-sought-after scholarship was an even more impressive achievement.

Although he had hoped that his time at Oxford would further help him become an author, Pullman never found the inspiration there that he was looking for. Having fallen in love with the place on first visiting it while still at school, he felt badly let down by the poor quality of the teaching he received there. Dull lectures and an absence of any seminars where he could learn from, and debate with, other students meant that his only teaching contact each week was one hour with a tutor who never seemed very inter-ested in the first place. Pullman grew increasingly restless with a system that demanded so much read-ing from one week to another while also providing so little time for adequate discussion.

4. Philip in top hat in *Doctor in the House*, aged sixteen. (Reproduced by kind permission of Philip Pullman.)

After a year he applied to join another course specialising in politics, philosophy and psychology. But his request was refused, and his final, disappointing, third-class degree was an indication of what can go wrong when a clever pupil is denied the sort of learning experience within which he or she can truly flourish. Pullman's often passionate engagement with educational issues since, and in particular his concern with what he sees as the dull and unimaginative ways of teaching the young now enshrined in the National Curriculum, could well date back to this time in his life. Excellent teaching at school which was then replaced by a university system where very little tuition of real value happened at all was enough to make anyone angry.

There were plenty of good times though, with some acting in drama groups and rather more folk-singing to his own guitar accompaniment. There was also 'a group of idle friends who occupied their time and mine betting on horses, getting drunk, and sprawling about telling creepy tales.' This life had something in common with Lyra's own time at Oxford, including her habit of crawling about on her college's roof:

> In my second year I occupied the rooms at the top of staircase 8, next to the lodge tower, and a friend, Jim Taylor, discovered that you could get out of the

window and crawl along a very useful gutter behind the parapet. From there you could climb in through another window further along. I gave Lyra a better head for heights than I have, but I did the gutter crawl a number of times, usually when there was a party on the next staircase.

During his last year at university, Pullman came across the plot description on the back of Mikhail Bulgakov's famous pre-war Russian novel *The Master and Margarita*. This read: 'One hot spring the devil

5. Exeter College, Oxford, on which the Jordan College of *His Dark Materials* is based. The doorway to staircase 8 is on the right of the main archway (in the centre of the photo).

arrives in Moscow accompanied by a retinue that includes a beautiful naked witch and an immense talking black cat with a fondness for chess and vodka.' Without wanting to read the actual book, in case it interfered with the workings of his own imagination, Pullman knew straightaway that this mixture of the ordinary and the fantastic was what he was looking for, and decided there and then to become a novelist himself. Starting to write his first book on a beautiful summer morning the day after he left university, Pullman got to around page 70 of a magical-realistic story before he was summoned out to Uganda to look after his mother who had become ill. He told himself that if he could still get to page 100, he would know that one day he would really become a proper author. Writing his three pages a day, a habit he has maintained ever since, he finally made his hundred pages before abandoning the story which he had now lost interest in, without even bothering to type it out.

With the vague idea of becoming a singer-songwriter, Pullman first worked in London at the famous gent's outfitters Moss Bros before trying his hand as an assistant librarian. A second novel followed, which won Pullman joint first prize in a literary competition designed for would-be writers below the age of 25. Described by Pullman as a metaphysical thriller, he now condemns this book as rubbish and wants nothing more to do with it. Finally

6. Philip in beret, aged twenty-five. (Reproduced by kind permission of Philip Pullman.)

training as a teacher, for the next twelve years he taught children between 9 and 13, both at the rough end of Oxford and also in a more middle-class area.

One of his jobs was to put on the school play, and soon he was writing the material himself, ranging from comic melodrama to ghost stories. These productions were always popular with parents as well as with pupils, giving Pullman his first hint that adults and children often enjoy the same sort of story so long as it is put over to them effectively. Turning the plays into published stories was a further step in his career as an author.

At his second school, Pullman had the job of stocking the school library. Initially he was doubtful whether the parents in this more traditional part of Oxford would be willing to embrace some of the new realism in teenage fiction that was at this time causing some controversy. Summoning six parents from all walks of life to a meeting, Pullman handed out some of the more outspoken titles he particularly respected, asking them to read each one carefully before deciding whether these were the sort of books they wanted for their children.

The results at their next meeting were extremely positive. Although occasionally shaken by the sometimes controversial choice of subject matter in this new writing, the parents all agreed that the authors in question were treating it sensitively and responsibly,

7. Philip, arms akimbo with walking stick, aged twenty-six. (Reproduced by kind permission of Philip Pullman.)

and that there would be no objections to such books appearing in the library. For Pullman, this was an extra-significant victory. It signalled to him that writing for the young was now free from many of the restrictions that once used to bear down on authors trying to tell teenagers the truth as they saw it. This realisation was another important step in his decision to become a children's novelist himself.

Still writing three pages a day, Pullman was by now regularly published, with his first fantasy and crime stories earning him enough to make it possible for him to change to a part-time job at Westminster College, Oxford, where he was Senior Lecturer in English. This job involved teaching prospective teachers, with Pullman specialising in a course on storytelling. Training young teachers how to put across stories to children in the most effective way, Pullman used to narrate favourite tales to them himself by way of an object lesson, concentrating particularly on Greek myths. The fearsome harpies of Homer's *Odyssey* are not the only figures from these great myths to make a later appearance in *His Dark Materials*. The constant re-visiting of these most famous of stories also further convinced Pullman of the appeal of narrative for all ages, when there is a clear plot and a lively sense of adventure – characteristics he was also to take into his own writing.

By now married and with two children, he would henceforth spend each writing day shutting himself away in his shed at the bottom of the garden which – like Roald Dahl before him – gave him the temporary, total isolation he needed for writing. He once said that if he were to have a dæmon – the type of animal guardian-angel found throughout *His Dark Materials* – it would probably be a jackdaw or a magpie. His description of the particular shed in

8. Philip with his son Jamie, in about 1980. (Reproduced by kind permission of Philip Pullman.)

which he writes gives some idea why these particular birds came to mind.

My shed is a twelve foot by eight foot wooden structure, with electricity, insulation, heating, a carpet, the table where I write (which is covered in an old kilim rug), my exorbitantly expensive Danish tilting-in-all-directions orthopaedic gas-powered swivelling chair, my old computer, printer and scanner (i.e. they don't work any more but I'm too mean to throw them out), manuscripts, drawings, apple cores, spiders' webs, dust, books in tottering heaps all over the floor and on every horizontal surface, about a thousand jiffy bags from books for review which I'm also too mean to throw away, a six-foot-long stuffed rat (the Giant Rat of Sumatra from a production of a Sherlock Holmes play I wrote for the Polka Theatre), a saxophone, a guitar, dozens of masks of one sort or another, piles and piles of books and more books and still more books, a heater, an old armchair filled to capacity with yet more books, a filing cabinet that I haven't managed to open for eighteen months because of all the jiffy bags and books which have fallen in front of it in a sort of landslide, more manuscripts, more drawings, broken pencils, sharpened pencils, dust, dirt, bits of chewed carpet from when my young pug Hogarth comes to visit, stones of every kind: a cobblestone from Prague, a bit of Mont Blanc, a bit of Cape

Cod … On and on the list goes. It is a filthy abominable tip. No-one would go in there unless they absolutely had to. I enter it each morning with reluctance and leave as soon as I can.

I have included this long quotation as it gives such a vivid impression of Pullman himself. Interested in everything that comes his way, self-deprecating but also very much his own master, quizzical, forthright and bursting with ideas, he is an excellent speaker as well as a brilliant writer. His enthusiasm even for the contents of his old shed is typical of his generally positive attitude towards the whole of life itself. He is also a generous man, always happy to praise those other children's authors that he reads and enjoys. When he writes in *His Dark Materials* that heaven should be seen not as another place but very much where we are at the moment, there is no doubt that he is also referring to the continual joy he finds in his own life. This is particularly true of his beloved family and his many interests over and above the immense satisfaction he draws from having written the books that he has.

Pullman is an emotional man, laughing, shuddering and on occasions weeping over his stories as they unfold. His main characters often seem to make their presence known to him suddenly and spontaneously. In the case of Lyra in *His Dark Materials*, he has said it was as if he could hear her voice and knew precisely what she looked like. He has strong opinions, but writes the books that he feels he must, with no intention of necessarily converting anyone else to his point of view. Left wing in his politics, he sees his writing as part of a dissenting tradition stretching back to his particular hero William Blake. He is also a skilled artist, providing the illustrations and chapter headings for all three parts of *His Dark Materials*.

A central part of Pullman's philosophy as a writer is that people should be judged by what they do rather than what they say. This rests upon another assumption, which is that since everyone always has the power of choice, it is up to them to see that they make the right ones. His own life could be seen as an example of someone who has chosen the positive rather than the negative path. An unsettled childhood involving constant moves, a succession of new schools, a dead father, a stepfather and an often absent mother could have been seen as reason for resentment, both at the time and possibly later on as well.

But Pullman has no such reservations, always choosing to celebrate the positive features of his life to date. For some, such optimism smacks of denial, with Pullman unwilling to register the anger and depression he might once have felt as a child, preferring instead to express it in his writing when it comes to portraying some of his most hated and generally hateful villains. For others, probably including Pullman himself, his life is a story within which the love of important others plus the powers of his own imagination have provided all that he ever needed, both as man and boy.

Taking the position that individuals – including himself – always have the power and ability to be ultimately responsible for the course of their own lives has been an important factor in enabling Pullman to write the positive stories that he has. This type of inner conviction, linked to his extraordinary powers of imagination, has succeeded in leaving multitudes of readers, both young and old, feeling better both about themselves and the various possibilities with which they are surrounded. This is a particular achievement at a time when there are many others, both in life and in literature, who take a far bleaker view of the power of any individual to shape their own lives to any significant degree at all.

This is additionally true in the sense that Pullman himself cannot simply be written off as one of those lucky enough to be born the type of optimist who can always find a positive in everything. He has also had experience of depression, which he has described as a time when 'life and the meaning and the colour drains out of everything and leaves you indifferent, indifferent to your own self as well as anyone else.' He says more about this in an interesting dialogue with Marie Bridge, as part of a series of conversations with authors and psychoanalysts held at the Institute of Psychoanalysis in January 2003 and due to be published later on in the same year.

The particular journeys his main characters have to take in order to arrive where they want to be are often hard and testing, requiring constant courage as well as an unwavering – though not unquestioning – faith in the whole enterprise at all stages. The temptation to give up at any time can only be countered by making a renewed effort, even in the toughest of conditions. If and when a particular battle is finally won, it may be at some personal cost. So although Pullman chooses a fantasy setting for his most important novels, his main characters still basically achieve their ends through hard work. The same could also be said of the author himself, shut away in his shed at the bottom of the garden and not allowing himself to leave until he has written the three pages per day that finally meet with his stringent and ever-demanding standards of artistic approval.

9. Philip Pullman, taken *c.* 1997. (Reproduced by permission of Scholastic Ltd.)

The Sally Lockhart
Novels

The Sally Lockhart Novels

Pullman has always been a great fan of Conan Doyle's famous Sherlock Holmes stories, reading them over and over again. He also still adores the adventure comics he so loved when young. As a former teacher of English in schools, he wanted to write a series of pacey, exciting novels that the children he had once taught might enjoy. The end result was four gripping books largely set in late nineteenth-century London, combining the traditional Victorian detective story with modern touches drawn from a whole range of popular film and fiction. Their plots race along, containing many scenes of huge excitement and suspense on the way. But Pullman also provides his own radical take on the social and political assumptions of that period, making sure that readers do a bit of thinking while enjoying the hectic action.

There are many references in these stories to often quaintly named Victorian inventions, some genuine, others made up. The street slang his characters speak also provides a similarly entertaining mixture of what was real and what Pullman has imagined. Repetition is avoided by having characters provide each other with numerous, instant summaries of what has happened when this is necessary for the plot, but always safely off the page so as not to hold things up. When it comes to disclosing something new and important, the same characters will often talk at great length and with no interruption until all they have to say has been thoroughly taken in.

Sally Lockhart, who begins the series as a sixteen-year-old orphan, is someone who has the uncomfortable but highly readable gift of attracting danger from all quarters. Some of these threats come from traditional sources that would also have been familiar to readers of the Sherlock Holmes stories, such as the villains of the blackest possible nature who cross her path. At other times she goes into the slums and opium dens of Victorian London, again at constant risk. But fortunately she is always supported by the band of loyal friends with whom she lives and works.

This small group is in turn helped out by gangs of children, expert in tracking, stealing and fighting but always honest when dealing with Sally and her friends. Sherlock Holmes also used to call on similar support from the street urchins of his own day, very useful when it comes to getting a sometimes dodgy job done with no awkward questions asked after-wards. The same is true in another novel Pullman greatly admires: Erich Kästner's pre-war children's classic, *Emil and the Detectives*. In this story, young Emil is helped by some friendly and ingenious Berlin children to track down the crook who had stolen his money. Talking about this book in a public lecture, Pullman has said its main point is 'that the children find the solution themselves, out of the everyday qualities they share: resourcefulness, quick wits, deter-mination.' The street urchins in his Sally Lockhart series are exactly the same, driving home Pullman's abiding belief in the inherent quality of all ordinary people, including children, if only they are given the chance to show it.

The stories in this series are told with great flare, using numbers of stock plot devices. Vital informa-tion is often overheard just when the need is greatest. Happy coincidences occur, and there is usually just enough money for everyone to get by, however little actual work sometimes seems to take place. Those in particular need of rescue and who don't know where to turn are regularly given shelter by Sally and her friends, just as the kindly Mr Brownlow in Charles Dickens's *Oliver Twist* unquestioningly takes in the young Oliver when he sees that he is ill and starving.

Such acts of charity did of course sometimes occur in real life. But there is a limit to the extent that well-meaning individuals can offer significant help, other than to just a few individuals, in those societies where there is already so much hardship that it is difficult to know where to start and whom to relieve first. The way that extreme poverty eventually brutalises everyone in real life is certainly something Pullman takes on in these stories. But he also believes that individuals can make important differences to an unjust society when it comes to inspiring and promoting political and social change. Sally and her friends meanwhile can always be relied on to do the right thing, however poor they may sometimes be themselves. The fact that their kindness and generosity never seems to come at any real cost in terms of subsequent emotional or financial problems is part of the romantic license found throughout these stories.

This is not to say that Pullman is like Dickens in suggesting that poverty could largely be got rid of if only a few more misers like Scrooge in *The Christmas Carol* became more charitable. He makes it clear that a total re-organisation of society is called for rather than a few more saintly child-savers. When left-wing Daniel Goldberg addresses oppressed, badly paid Londoners at a public meeting in *The Tiger in the Well*, he makes the case for a living wage, decent housing and social justice which Pullman clearly believes in for himself. Sally starts out by accepting the way that society is but finishes by believing that ruthless capitalism is the greatest evil of all. She also has to accept that by owning shares in companies she now knows to be corrupt she is contributing directly to such evil herself.

Sally goes on to have a baby while she is still unmarried. She makes no apology for what would have been a considerable scandal in her own day, glorying in her small daughter. Here as elsewhere, she makes the case for liberated women by living a liberated life herself. When her lover Frederick Garland tries at various times to offer her his full protection, he is angrily dismissed. After his death, when she is threatened with being separated from her baby as well as with losing all her money, Pullman reveals the full horror of the way that Victorian men stood to take over everything that belonged to their wives immediately after marriage. When Sally is condemned as a prostitute after her illegitimate baby is born, the hypocrisy of a society that prefers to stick with stuffy conventions rather than recognise an act of true love is obvious for all to see.

The first story, *The Ruby in the Smoke*, began as a play written for pupils when Pullman was still a teacher. It starts with typical fizz, as if daring readers not to give up after such an arresting opening. In the second paragraph of the first page, we are told of Sally Lockhart that 'within fifteen minutes, she was going to kill a man.' And so she does, although not on purpose. Shortly after that she meets the main cast of players for this and the other three stories in the series: Frederick Garland, a photographer but also a brilliant and fearless detective, Rosa, his fiery sister, Jim Taylor, an office boy with a talent for scrapping, and Trembler Molloy, an ex-pickpocket now turned general help. Staying on first as lodger and then as the accountant for this little group, Sally 'found herself wondering what it was that was so unusual about this household.' The answer comes to her just as she is getting into bed. 'They don't think of Trembler as a servant. And they don't think of me as a girl. We're all equal. That's what's so odd.'

Even odder are the adventures that follow, with Sally in possession of information that could lead to the discovery of one of the world's most valuable rubies. Cursed from the time it was first stolen, this jewel finally proves more trouble than it is worth. But before it delivers its final consignment of ill fortune, there are numbers of dramatic plot twists. Sally discovers the name of her real father, tries to rescue Adelaide Bevan, an abused servant child, and at close range shoots the villainous Ah Ling, a Chinese Mr Big who deals in adulterated opium and has always wanted the ruby for himself.

She also has the satisfaction of seeing the foul old lady who murdered her father fall to her death in pursuit of the deadly ruby. Finally she learns the terrible truth about the opium trade, and the way that former British governments had forced the Chinese to deal in it at the cost of two so-called Opium Wars. This disgraceful act was until comparatively recently often passed over in school lessons and textbooks, and still remains a little-known part of British colonial history.

The Shadow in the North continues the same pattern of mixing nostalgic references to past popular fiction with modern social attitudes. Against a colourful background of music-hall entertainers, spiritualist sessions and experiments in early photography, a hugely evil villain has somehow to be stopped before committing the ultimate wickedness – in this case, making available on the international market the Steam Gun, a horrible new weapon of mass destruction. He has previously made some of his vast fortune from owning match factories, and there are numbers of references to the dreadful industrial injuries suffered by the workers in such places.

Great play is also made of Jim, the office boy, and his love of the lurid comics and plays he so enjoys and also tries to write. But while the plot of this novel is at times equally melodramatic, Pullman distances himself from many of the clichés found in turn-of-the-century romances. When Frederick and Jim take on a hired thug called Sackville, they fight every way they can, for 'as far as Jim was concerned, anything you did in a fight was fair, because if you didn't do it, the other bugger would, so you might as well do it first.' The language here would have been totally unacceptable in even the most sensationalist penny-dreadful magazine in Jim's library at the time, which would also have insisted that a truly British hero would by definition always fight fair. Later on, Jim weeps at the death of Frederick. As he realises himself, although 'men didn't cry in the fiction Jim read and wrote, they did in real life all right.'

The issue of mass poverty is also raised again, most acutely, by Axel Bellmann, the Swedish arms-dealing villain. He argues that it does not matter if he is producing a genuinely evil weapon if all the workers involved in its production are happy and comparatively well paid. This is very similar to the arguments found in George Bernard Shaw's play *Major Barbara*. The plight of those middle-class idealists in Pullman's stories who don't realise that their income derives from slum landlords also looks back to other plays by Shaw, such as *Widowers' Houses* and *Mrs Warren's Profession*. Although tired and confused, Sally finally summons up the courage to confront Bellmann. 'They hate the Steam Gun, your workers. They know what it means, and they loathe it. You keep it secret because you're afraid of what people would think if they knew – that's the only reason. You know the British people wouldn't stand for it if they saw it clearly for what it is – a tyrant's weapon, a coward's weapon.'

This type of resoundingly patriotic declaration was once common in adventure stories written for younger audiences. But in a sign of the greater complexity still to come in his writing, Pullman allows Bellmann to have not just the last word but also the better of the argument. 'These British people you mention; shall I tell you the truth? If they knew, they wouldn't mind. They'd have no scruples about making the most horrible weapon ever invented. … Reality is with me. I promised you the truth: there it is.' Faced by this cynicism, Sally is momentarily at a loss, and in the next chilling and unexpected sentence, Pullman adds 'She knew he was right.' Is Pullman thinking here of the various repulsive weapons, bombs and mines that continue to be made by British companies right up to our own time?

This does not stop Sally from finally destroying the Steam Gun and Bellmann in the process. In their last confrontation, she declares 'You're wrong, because you don't understand loyalty, you don't understand love … the world you want to create is based on fear and deception and murder and lies.' Even so, she has come close enough to him to experience his almost electrical energy. After his somewhat improbable offer of marriage, along with kisses charged with a sulphurous crackle, Sally is forced to discover at first

THE GIPSY OF ROSEMARY DELL.

overed her mistake, and scarcely knowing which way it would be best or her to proceed, or whether she should turn back.

10. Four illustrations from Victorian penny dreadfuls.
The melodrama of the penny dreadful is well captured

tempted to drag her away, while Susan wrung her hands and screamed loudly for help

by Pullman's *Sally Lockhart* novels. (Reproduced by permission of the British Library.)

hand the terrible attraction that can be held out by ultimate evil when presented in its most seductive form. This theme crops up again in *His Dark Materials*.

Sally's reference to love is especially poignant, since by now she and Frederick had pledged themselves to each other after a troubled courtship. But Frederick is also killed by Bellmann, just as he has killed so many others who happened to get in his way. When Sally in her turn slays Bellmann at the same time as blowing up his beloved Steam Gun, she intends to die as well, such is her grief. But then she discovers that she is carrying Frederick's child, and finishes her story on a note of joyful expectation, backed up by all those closest to her. By contrast, Bellmann, interested only in power for himself and the potential for power in the wife of his choice, could never have understood love simply for its own sake. But love for the good and true in someone else, and the way it can make any life truly worthwhile, is another important theme in Pullman's novels.

In *The Tiger in the Well*, the best of this series so far, Sally is now the mother of Harriet, a delightful little girl close on two years old. But, when a plot is hatched to steal her away with the full backing of the law, Harriet also turns out to be Sally's weakest link. This situation arises when a man she has never met claims to be Sally's husband and sues her for divorce. Sally's initial response is to go out and buy a pistol. But things get too much and she is forced to go into hiding. By this time her mysterious 'husband' has seized all her money and goods, which he was legally permitted to do as the so-called aggrieved party. Living in poverty and squalor for the first time, Sally at last gets to know about the terrible life lived by so many other 'poor, anonymous people. They were only anonymous because of her own ignorance; they each had a life inside them, just as she did.'

Previously describing herself as a capitalist with no time for any notions of socialism, Sally now has a change of mind. Facing the realities of trying to live a decent life in appalling housing, symbolised here by the presence of only one single, blocked lavatory supposed to serve eight over-crowded dwellings, she pledges herself to fight for the rights of everyone else in similar circumstances. As she puts it at the end of this story, 'There was much for her to do. Not single-handedly; she'd learned that lesson. Things got done in the world when you worked with other people. There were movements to join, things to learn, groups to organise, speeches to make.' Now that the threat to her child is lifted, following the collapse of the plot against her, there will be more time for such activities.

She has also decided to marry Daniel Goldberg, the Jewish socialist orator who came to her aid when she most needed it. A revolutionary but not a terrorist, it is he who opens Sally's eyes to the need for social change. What he advocates is now taken for granted but was still fairly new and strange in 1881, the time when this novel is set. It is Goldberg who tells Sally about the desperate scramble men had to get a job in the London Docks each day, with sadistic foremen sometimes setting them up to fight each other for a place. It is he who tells her about the white slave trade, where poor Jewish immigrant girls are told a few lies and then whisked away to a life of prostitution almost always ending in an early death.

Sally also learns a good deal for herself, including the lesson that people living in poverty often come to fear each other too, when life is little more than a fight for the survival of the fittest. Some of the tricks played on newly arrived immigrants by local inhabitants in this story are particularly mean, such as the cabbies who offer them rides to somewhere far away and then charge them a fortune. Clearly there's a long way to go before everyone has the chance to live the sort of life that makes it unnecessary for them to prey on others. But having shown that the evil which arises between people is often caused by poverty and injustice, Pullman also produces a villain who is pure evil through and through. Enter once more the infamous Ah Ling from *The Ruby in the Smoke*, now totally paralysed from Sally's pistol shot but still determined to ruin her life.

Their last show-down arrives when Ah Ling tries to

kill Sally and is then nearly saved by her from his own death. But having got so close to reality in his descriptions of the appalling conditions in London's East End, there is something unsatisfying in the way that Pullman brings on such a very old-fashioned villain. In true comic book style, Ah Ling looks repulsive, behaves melodramatically and lives outside any recognisable social context. With his arrival on the scene, the strain of combining social realism with popular fantasy begins to show, with the set-piece description of Ah Ling's spectacular death less convincing the longer it goes on.

The last book in this series to date, *The Tin Princess*, is the least successful. The story is almost pure romance, with any nods in the direction of reality limited to the first few pages. Starting off with sixteen-year-old Becky in search of a job as a language tutor, the action soon moves to the tiny and imaginary country of Razkavia, squeezed between German and Austria, both of which have designs upon some valuable nickel mines. The Princess of this country is none other than Adelaide Bevan, the cockney child last heard of in *The Ruby in the Smoke*. Things had at first gone hard for her after that time, and she has had to endure a spell of enforced prostitution. But now she seems to have struck it lucky by marrying one of her former clients, Crown Prince Rudolph. Unfortunately there are also constant plots against the Razkavian royal family both in Britain and in Razkavia. First the old King is murdered and soon after that the Prince is killed as well. Left on her own, the new Queen quickly enlists help from Jim Taylor, also one of the original group. Although their efforts to save the little country fail, Adelaide makes a splendid monarch. Resourceful as ever, Jim is always by her side, and it is no surprise when they decide to marry in the closing pages.

There is little this time about the sort of social conditions witnessed and condemned by Sally in the previous stories. Indeed, Sally and her politically active husband make very little appearance at all. Razkavia itself is certainly full of political intrigue, but it is hard to get too engaged in the doings of a purely imaginary country. Adelaide makes another stand for women and what they can achieve; she also demon-strates that her working-class background and lack of education are no handicaps to the development of a lively intelligence. But when she is shown as capable of overseeing a complicated treaty between Razkavia and its neighbours despite having only just learned to read, belief becomes strained. Her uncomplicated reactionary views also remain uncontested in a way that would not have happened in the previous books.

Other elements in this story also jar. Ancient comic-book clichés now crop up unchallenged. Jim decides to trust a young man he has just met on the questionable grounds that 'I've seen the way you fight.' Later on, when Prince Rudolph has doubted his loyalty, he comes up with a speech that reads like a parody of old-fashioned British-is-best patriotism. 'I'm an Englishman, by God, and I'll thank you to remember it. I'm not bribed by treaties or bullied by threats, and I won't be bought by gold.'

Elsewhere, eyes flash, mouths purse and bosoms heave as Pullman continues with a largely uncritical use of old stereotypes. At the end of the story, the fighting between the various camps is as lovingly described as any of the battles in the Narnia stories of C.S. Lewis that Pullman so dislikes. When Jim desperately defends Adelaide after she has been laid low by a bullet, he is described approvingly as 'fighting the air itself, hacking, slicing, cutting, thrusting.' This is closer to traditional adventure film heroics than to real life, and it is noticeable that while all the main characters receive injuries in this book, there is no real feeling for the actual pain and suffering that follow from serious wounds.

Only in the last few pages is there anything like the deeper discussion found in the other three books. When Jim is convinced that he is about to die in the battle to save the Razkavian flag, he wonders how exactly he got to this position. He is quite unable to find a consistent thread between what his life has been up to that moment and what he is experiencing now. Instead, 'There was no pattern in things, Jim saw, no sense; everything was random and chaotic. Which left a ragged band of wounded people struggling to plant a rectangle of silk in a heap of ruins, and die defending it. Since nothing made sense, that made as much sense as anything else.'

This is not the final word. When Sally meets Becky, she tells her that although superior force usually wins at the time, just as it did in the obliteration of Razkavia by its more powerful German neighbour, people will eventually 'want to take charge of their own destiny again. Life's not static, you see, Becky. Life's dynamic. Everything changes. That's the beauty of it.' Sally herself provides good evidence of this. 'She was so much the kind of woman Becky wanted to be; she showed it was *possible*; she brought hope with her, and a sense of wide, continuing, bustling life.' So while the latest Sally Lockhart novel still ends on a note of affirmation, the former ideal of social action is now joined by an equal emphasis on individual fulfilment, also one of Pullman's favourite themes.

Although *The Tin Princess* sets out to be a realistic story, there are times when readers could well think they are in a work of outright fantasy. The character of Carmen Ruiz, the crazed Spanish wife of Prince Rudolph's mad older brother, is a case in point. Unbelievably strong, surviving against impossible odds, always up for one more murderous assault, she is more supernatural than real. There are also glimpses in the other novels of a leaning away from realism towards straight fantasy. *The Shadow in the North* has the character Nellie Budd, a fake spiritualist medium who is also a genuine clairvoyant with the power to reveal past secrets in close and accurate detail. Such claims have often been made in real life, but even so there has never been anyone so far quite as effortlessly effective as Mrs Budd, who in this story is shown recalling vital incidents from the past at length and in considerable detail.

The same is true of Alistair Mackinnon, a dislike-able Scottish conjurer also able at a moment's notice to re-create accurate images from the past simply by holding an associated object such as a cigar case. This skill does him no good, when it leads him to discovering the identity of a murderer who then wants him killed before this dangerous information gets out. Once again, Mackinnon's amazing ability to bring back the past goes far beyond anything ever claimed by or for real life clairvoyants. Instead, the various descriptions of his mysterious powers look forward to similar skills possessed by some of the main characters in *His Dark Materials*, also able to read either the past or the future at various stages.

Pullman has said in an interview that he would like to write more books in this series. 'I like these characters, I like the way they interact with each other, and I want to see more of Jim and Adelaide in particular. I want to bring the events up to the mid-1890s before I've finished.' One reason for choosing this date is that it was the time when the first true moving pictures began to be shown on the screen. The development of photography is one of the main themes in this series, and one of particular interest to Pullman. He has always believed that photography relates closely to story-telling, with pictures standing in for words. In 1896 Sally's daughter Harriet would be sixteen, when it could be time for her to start having adventures as well.

Detective stories written for younger readers often tend to fall into two camps. There are those that take themselves very seriously, usually involving young sleuths well ahead of the adult world when it comes to following up clues and even making final arrests, to general praise all round. High on reader flattery if low on credibility, this type of fantasy is still best represented in the *Famous Five* and *Secret Seven* series written by Enid Blyton during and after the last war, although there have been many other imitations since.

Another popular type of junior detective story sticks to the theme of young people outwitting older, criminal ones, but this time plays up the humour implicit in the situation. The young sleuths in these stories often get most things wrong, and frequently have to be bailed out by generally disapproving parents or teachers. Occasionally their suspicions are based on a complete misunderstanding of what has been happening, with any final unmasking of adult villains as much a matter of luck as design. Good-humoured rather than going in for over-the-top heroics, these stories also regularly end on a happy note for all concerned.

Pullman's Sally Lockhart stories steer a path between these two extremes, finishing up with something more substantial while always remaining exciting and entertaining. His main players are no longer young children, and many of them have to cope with typical adult concerns. Each book starts with something of a cliché, such as a cursed gem stone, a villain out to destroy the world or a teenager suddenly becoming a member of a royal family. But what happens after that gets closer to realism than is usually the case in stories falling back upon such well-worn stereotypes. It is as if Pullman is revisiting the comic-strip adventures of his youth while also bringing to them a general fascination with the social history of the time. This is not simply a matter of describing the various inventions that would once have seemed so revolutionary. The struggle for social justice and reform also plays a large part in these stories. To the extent that some of the social issues he describes still remain unresolved today, these books continue to concern the present as well as the past.

In *The Ruby in the Smoke*, Sally discovers that the man she thought of as her father had in fact adopted her. She has no knowledge of her mother; a situation that crops up in a number of Pullman's novels. But she is troubled by terrifying memories of her own past that she can't make any sense of. There is a lot therefore for her to find out, and this quest for self-knowledge on the part of the main character has often formed an important part of some of the greatest adventure stories of all time. It is a theme that Pullman keeps returning to in his later writing.

Other Stories

Introduction

Pullman has always remained fond of *Galatea*, his first published adult novel. A magical-realist story before its time, it never achieved large sales but still reads well today. Its main character is Mark Browning, a flautist living in Valencia who, coming home one morning, finds that his beloved wife has disappeared. His search for her leads him to Venezuela, where he encounters a strange organisation known as the Anderson Valley Project. This is worked by Zombies, which means there are never problems with having to pay any wages.

The next city he discovers has inhabitants who are immortal since they live off electricity and have no blood. It is also full of hideous mutations, the work of some skilled but barbarous surgeons. In an argument with a bishop who happens to be there, Browning tells him that 'Good works alone are the measure of goodness.' Any alternative idea that suffering can also lead to goodness is 'the doctrine of Hell.' The idea that goodness concerns what people do rather than what they are is a central one in Pullman's later novels, and it is interesting to see it cropping up here as well. There are other passages where characters argue with each other about how to establish a civilisation that would actually be worth something. Such flashes of moral earnestness inserted between other moments of high adventure are also to be found in Pullman's work still to come.

There are other glimpses of the direction Pullman was to take. The book's cast includes zombies, mutants, werewolves and the ghosts not just of people but also of objects and animals. All these characters testify to an imagination already willing to go the extra distance into another world of fantasy. Pullman's characteristic sympathy with the poor and oppressed is also evident in his description of a successful slave revolt, led by Browning himself. Browning finally arrives at a third city, also inhabited by unreal people, where he falls in love with a beautiful automaton – the Galatea of the title. Eventually he returns home and, somewhat to his surprise, becomes a millionaire. Pullman would surely have been astonished at the time had anyone suggested that a similar fate would await him too after years more of writing.

Illustrated Fiction

*C*ount Karlstein, or the Ride of the Demon Huntsman, Pullman's first children's novel, grew from a play he had written and produced while he was a teacher. In a new author's note to this story he says that putting on the original production was the greatest fun he had ever known in his life. All the ingredients that make for instant popularity with young audiences are there: ghosts, slapstick and numbers of special effects. When something went wrong in one performance the pupil actors were able to come up with improvised lines on their own account in order to put everything right.

Set in Switzerland in 1816, the story starts with Hildi spinning her brother Peter a terrifying story about a Demon Huntsman. Telling such tales is something they do every night once they are safely in bed, just as Pullman himself used to with his brother when they were both young. Hildi herself continues as the main narrator for the rest of the book, although other characters take up the tale from time to time. High melodrama rules throughout, involving orphaned fugitives, a wicked uncle and numbers of narrow escapes. Typical of other Pullman heroines in the future, Hildi is tough, brave and extremely resourceful. She also has a strong sense of right and wrong, and a belief that 'good should be done for its own sake and for nothing else.'

Packed with incident, this slight but energetic story also lays down some interesting markers for Pullman's career as a writer. A sense of the supernatural is never far away, with Zamiel, the ghostly spirit of the woods, at one point making an actual appearance. He inspires the sort of fear younger readers have always also enjoyed in their books simply because it is so remote from the realities of everyday existence. Closer to home, cruel Count Karlstein represents the type of mean, self-centred ruthlessness Pullman particularly loathes in real life. In contrast, younger characters come over as pleasant, courageous and happy to do the right thing. But they are also vulnerable to those older people who want to take advantage of them for their own evil ends. This ever-present threat to the young at a time in their lives when it is hard for them to defend themselves is also a theme Pullman was to return to.

The current edition of this book, appearing in 2002, backs away from the generous use of illustrations provided by Patrice Aggs in the 1991 edition.

These gave the whole work the look of a graphic novel, always one of Pullman's particular enthusiasms. The list of characters in this earlier edition included 'a suit of armour' and 'a bear's head'. A note about 'works consulted and ideas stolen from' included references from Janet and Allan Ahlberg's *Jolly Postman* series to The Swiss Police Handbook. Made-up titles in the list range from *Adeline, or the Skeleton Bride*, supposedly by Mrs Beeton, to two imaginary novels by his then editors: *Valloni, or The Spectre of the Lake* by Annie Eaton and *Rudolph, or The Hermit of the Forest* by David Fickling.

All this serves as a reminder of the origins of the book first as a children's play and then as a rumbustious story in the tradition of the full-scale melodrama once found in pantomime, early film and comic-strip magazines at their most uninhibited. The same type of over-the-top pastiche is also evident in Pullman's later re-telling of *Puss in Boots*, sub-titled *The Adventures of That Most Enterprising Feline* and illustrated by Ian Beck. The main cast is announced on the title page as if by a fanfare of invisible trumpets:

Starring PUSS himself, and featuring: One OGRE* Three GHOULS* One Aged and Respectable HERMIT****A Beautiful PRINCESS (Daughter of his most Gallic Majesty)****The KING OF FRANCE****And of course JACQUES, The Hero.

11. Patrice Agg's final spread from the illustrated version of *Count Karlstein* (Philip Pullman, *Count Karlstein, or the Ride of the Demon Huntsman*, Corgi Yearling, 1991. Illustrations copyright © 1991 Patrice Aggs. Reproduced by permission of A.P. Watt Ltd on behalf of Patrice Aggs.)

The text itself is packed with illustrations of different sizes, speech bubbles, jokes, mock letters and visiting cards, and is also based on a play written by Pullman for the Polka Theatre, which specialises in drama aimed at young people. It all makes for excellent fun, and a reminder that although Pullman deals seriously with serious topics, he is also someone who enjoys literary play simply for its own sake. Jokes, pastiche, irony and nostalgia for past books, films and comics all play an important part in his works, and particularly in his shorter stories for younger children. This capacity for sheer enjoyment in what he is doing enabled him first to become an effective playwright for children. Transferred into his books, and helped on by able illustrators and typesetters with an eye for the dramatic, it then played an important part in his success as a story-teller whose obvious enjoyment in what he is doing helps make his books equally enjoyable to other readers in turn.

Spring-Heeled Jack: A Story of Bravery and Evil (1989) also grew from a play written at school for his pupils, and is the closest Pullman has got to the complete graphic novel that he would one day like both to write and illustrate. It is a high-spirited romp, with frequent references to old Victorian penny dreadfuls and modern comics like the *Beano* and *Dandy* that Pullman enjoyed when young. Mean orphanage superintendents rub shoulders with wicked crooks like Mack the Knife, 'the most evil villain in London.' But neither can withstand Spring-Heeled Jack – a sort of good devil turned superman, with powers of flight and a strong desire to put right serious wrongs. The story is told in both words and pictures, provided in this case by David Mostyn in true comic-book style. For fans of *His Dark Materials*, there is a foretaste of dæmons with the appearance on page 38 of a 'bedraggled little creature like a mournful moth.' Looking like a tiny middle-aged man, he sits on the shoulder of Filthy, one of Mack the Knife's gang, and acts as his highly unwelcome but persistent conscience.

Thunderbolt's Waxwork, is the first of two books featuring the New Cut Gang – a close-knit collection of mostly male children living in Lambeth, South London, in 1894, a date exactly a hundred years before this novel was published. Its main character, Thunderbolt Dobney, acquired this name after he had knocked out Crusher Watkins, leader of the rival Lower Marsh Gang. The reason for this fight was that Crusher had said something wounding about Thunderbolt's mother, who had recently died.

Like a junior version of the Sally Lockhart novels, there is plenty of period detail in this story linked to set pieces of high excitement as the gang sets about solving a mystery involving forged coins. One of them has already done a job the previous year for Sexton

Blake – a fictional detective in the tradition of Pullman's beloved Sherlock Holmes, and referred to here as if he were a real person. His superior sleuthing skills seem to have rubbed off on the gang itself, which finally come through with the answer to the main mystery, although not without various thrills and spills on the way.

The intention throughout is to amuse rather than educate, with a detective story plot that becomes amiably less likely as the action proceeds. Meeting in their own den in a stable yard, the gang has much in common with Richmal Crompton's famous stories featuring William Brown, which Pullman would certainly have enjoyed as a boy. Always coming up with unlikely ideas, disrespectful of adult authority including the local policeman, given to switching between grinning cheerfully, scowling in contempt or sighing in despair, William and Thunderbolt are alike in numbers of ways, even down to the type of fractured English with which they harangue their respective gangs.

Where they differ is over the quality of their home life. While William lives in a prosperous home-county village with his sorely tried parents, Thunderbolt only has his father who is always battling against poverty. William is expert in winding up his parents, but Thunderbolt feels generally protective towards his brilliantly inventive but otherwise disorganised

Pa, whom he has been looking after for a year since his mother died. When his father is arrested for forgery, Thunderbolt knows for certain that he is innocent. Reunited towards the end of the story, they hug each other as Thunderbolt weeps with relief. This is a level of emotion that Richmal Crompton would never have allowed herself to reach in her William stories, written only to entertain. But father-and-son relationships, when they do exist in Pullman's work, are never treated lightly, and the various separations between them that occur in his fiction are described with sadness rather than flippancy.

The Gas-Fitters' Ball continues with the adventures of the New Cut Gang, this time focusing on Benny Kaminsky, another of its members. Dreamy, often living in a world of his own, he unsuccessfully attempts to pass unnoticed in a laughable disguise complete with burned-cork moustache. At several stages gang members try to aid their older friend Dick Smith in his courtship of the attractive Daisy Miller. But they are quite as inept as any of the various attempts made by William and his gang of Outlaws to help out Robert and Ethel Brown, his long-suffering older siblings, in their many affairs of the heart.

As before, there are some nice period touches, in this case involving late-Victorian music halls and the early days of gas-fitments in general. Two more masterful little girls are now also part of the gang, and prove as effective as any of the boys there. The timely appearance of an unusually interested and hands-on Prince of Wales finally helps solve a major theft while also adding its own comic seal of cheerful implausibility. This is not a great book, but it is certainly a very jolly one, whose cockney capers invite readers to laugh both at and with its main juvenile characters. Young readers, who want to share this wish-fulfilment world within which children spot clues that everyone else has missed and so eventually solve a crime, will find plenty to entertain them both here and in the previous story about the ever-resilient New Cut Gang.

The Firework-Maker's Daughter, also enjoyed by younger readers, is another undemanding, feel-good story, this time featuring Lila, a typically sparky Pullman heroine in more ways than one. Unable to become a recognised firework-maker because she is a girl, she still triumphs thanks to her courage, determination and willpower. Lavishly illustrated, this time by Nick Harris, this lively story also includes a band of hopelessly inefficient pirates, a talking white elephant named Hamlet, and a terrifying visit to the Grotto of the Fire-Fiend himself. Winner of the Smarties Book Prize for its constant entertainment value, it has since been successfully adapted for the stage.

Yet again there are some serious moments in

between comic interludes involving the white elephant being used as a walking advertising hoarding and the pirates on their boat *The Bloody Murderer* behaving like over-grown schoolboys. Lila's relationship with her father is both affectionate and troubled, since while she wants to have a career he is only interested in finding her a husband. Once in the Grotto of Fire, Lila encounters a procession of ghosts who, in their weeping and wailing, anticipate the haunted spirits later found in *His Dark Materials*. In her encounter with Razvani, the great Fire-Fiend, Lila learns that the terrible flames surrounding him are not dangerous at all. Like Siegfried in the ancient story of the Nibelungs that Wagner later drew on for his opera cycle *The Ring*, Lila discovers that talent, courage and a moderate degree of luck can always defeat such deception, however dangerous it may seem.

This lesson is underlined by Razvani himself. 'Fire burns away all our illusions. The World itself is all illusion. Everything that exists flickers like a flame for a moment, and then vanishes. The only thing that lasts is change itself.' Even so, the finishing firework contest where Lila and her father triumph over stiff opposition is a reminder that a purely temporary display of great beauty, while it lasts, can still have the power to live on in the memory for ever. This skilful story, whose various plot twists gradually unfurl in different directions but still manage to come together in a final climax, reaches a quiet but satisfying conclusion – rather like the end of a successful firework display itself.

Clockwork, or All Wound Up, illustrated by Peter Bailey, is one of Pullman's best short books for younger children. Set in the same mid-European, mid-nineteenth-century world of *Count Karlstein*, it is a splendidly spooky tale involving Fritz, the village storyteller, a murderous wind-up model and a young prince with a mechanical heart that is gradually rusting away. He is finally saved by Gretl, the innkeeper's daughter, who by giving him her love enables the Prince to develop a real heart of his own. The wind-up model, meanwhile, is destroyed by the old clockmaker Herr Ringelmann, but not before it murders the sullen apprentice Karl, who was planning to use the robot to make himself rich.

Because Karl enters into a pact with the devil, represented here by the sinister Dr Kalmenius, he eventually dies a horrible death himself. The author adds that since this character also possessed a wicked heart, his bad end was well deserved. Karl in this sense is rather like Goethe's Faust, who also sold his soul to the devil but then wished that he had not. Dr Kalmenius wins him over by telling him that together they will be able to control the future. Just as a clock once wound up has no choice but to obey, so too can they now control destiny itself. 'Say to yourself: I *will* win that race – I *will* come first – and you wind up the future like clockwork. The world has no choice but to obey!'

During the eighteenth-century Sir Isaac Newton popularised a somewhat similar model of a mechanistic universe within which one scientific event will always necessarily follow another when the same conditions apply. But since the development of quantum mechanics at the beginning of the last century, scientists now take a much less deterministic view of why things happen as they do. Pullman is up to date with all these intellectual changes, including the contribution from quantum theory. This has taken the notion of the inherent instability of all matter and used it to suggest that there will always be a level of uncertainty when it comes to understanding the world we live in. At a moral level, Pullman also rejects the idea that humans are necessarily destined to act in a certain way. His belief in the power of choice is central to his whole moral philosophy.

So it is not surprising that in one of the boxes scattered throughout the text Pullman makes light work of the particular temptation held out by Dr Kalmenius to Karl of a time when he will be able to get anything he wants simply by wishing it. As Pullman sees it, 'you don't win races by wishing, you win them by running faster than everyone else. And to do that you have to train hard and strive your utmost, and sometimes even that isn't enough, because another runner just might be more talented than you are.'

But Pullman then follows up this sobering dose of realism with a more optimistic sentence: 'if you want something, you *can* have it, but only if you want everything that goes with it, including all the hard work and the despair, and only if you're willing to risk failure.' (p. 36) This does not quite add up, since if the end result may still be failure, it's hard to reconcile this with the idea that we can still always get what we want as long as we try hard enough.

It is also interesting that Pullman condemns Fritz for not finishing the story he begins telling the assembled villagers before he is interrupted by the dramatic entrance of Dr Kalmenius. For Pullman, 'Fritz was only playing at being a storyteller. If he was a proper craftsman like a clockwork-maker he'd have known that all actions have their consequences. For every tick there is a tock.' And later on, when Karl is about to be murdered by the robot he has given life to, Pullman apologises to his readers for this unpleasantness, telling them that 'I'd save the wretch if I could, but the story is wound up, and it must all come out.' So while we have choices in life, Pullman seems to be suggesting that in storytelling things must take a predestined course once the narrator has introduced his or her main characters. These will then follow their own paths, in the sense that these same characters then demand to act in their particular way.

Other modern writers often give their characters more room to manoeuvre, sometimes inviting readers into the actual telling of the story as it goes along and occasionally providing them with more than one ending. In such stories, readers may be required to work out for themselves what may have been going on in the spaces deliberately left for them to do so. The individual voice of the writer here can on occasions become another character in its own right. But at other times, the author may take his or her individual voice out of the narrative as much as is possible, leaving more room for a reader's own interpretation of a text.

But Pullman is something of an old-fashioned author when it comes to more experimental techniques in fiction. His whole approach is in distinct contrast to the way that some other writers for children now prefer to tell their stories more elliptically. Pullman is the opposite, always happy to put over his own views clearly and forcefully, either in his own right as author or more frequently through the mouths of his main characters. He also much prefers to tell stories where everyone, writer and reader alike, remains clear about what exactly is happening.

There is room for all sorts of narrative techniques in fiction; the fact that Pullman chooses to use one that has more in common with Dickens than with twentieth-century authors like Virginia Woolf is entirely his right. The fact too that his writing has proved so popular with adults as well as with children suggests that the thirst for stories written with a firm and unambiguous narrative voice remains as strong as ever.

Pullman also passes on some of his various opinions in the separate boxes scattered throughout this text within which he talks directly to readers about clockwork figures in general, the artistic temperament, the soul, winning and losing, doctors, wolves and anything else that takes his fancy. These boxes are rather like those odd facts or digressions that teachers sometimes slip into their lessons in order to keep pupils interested. They suggest what a good teacher Pullman must have been himself, whatever his occasional denials since.

Addressing readers directly is a technique also found in former children's writers such as Roald Dahl and C.S. Lewis. Although Pullman differs greatly from both of these in terms of his outlook, he has much in common with them as a particular type of storyteller. Like them, he writes in the main tradition of children's literature, spelling out characters and plot while always conveying a strong moral philosophy at the same time. Again like them, he has brought new life to this tried and tested formula which, while

ADVERTISEMENT

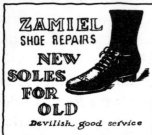

12. Patrice Agg's Advertisement appears at the back of the illustrated version of *Count Karlstein* (Philip Pullman, *Count Karlstein, or the Ride of the Demon Huntsman*, Corgi Yearling, 1991. Illustrations copyright © 1991 Patrice Aggs. Reproduced by permission of A.P. Watt Ltd on behalf of Patrice Aggs.)

not being the only way to tell a story, still remains the most popular and accessible way of doing so.

I Was a Rat!, or The Scarlet Slippers is the latest book for younger readers written by Pullman to date, and certainly one of his best. An ingenious mixture of fairy tale and Victorian melodrama, it is the first of his books to have been made into a full-length film. Its main character is one of the rats in the story of *Cinderella* who was changed into a pageboy but never managed to regain his original animal form. Like many other authors, Pullman is drawn to the Cinderella story, writing a similar version of it in *Mossycoat*, where he retells essentially the same plot in a different folk-tale setting. But *I Was a Rat!* provides a quite new take on this famous tale, so much so that readers often only become aware of its traditional roots during the last few pages.

The former rat's story starts hopefully enough, when he is fostered by kindly Bob the cobbler and his warm-hearted wife Joan. But after he is kidnapped by an unscrupulous circus showman, things grow worse. Escaping from this dreadful captor, he then, like Dickens' famous character Oliver Twist, comes under the influence of a band of young robbers and is taught how to steal. Urged on by the lying and sensationalist newspaper *The Daily Scourge*, the public allows itself to become persuaded that it is a thoroughly good thing when the rat boy is finally condemned to death as a self-evident monster. Only the intervention of the newly married Princess Aurelia saves his life at the last moment.

This Princess is in fact the former Cinderella, originally called here plain Mary Jane. She had known the rat boy when he was a genuine rodent which she used to feed in the kitchen where she worked all day. She now begs him to keep her secret, since no one else knows about her humble origin. But sad to say, she is beginning to wonder whether being a princess is all it is cracked up to be. As she explains to the rat boy, 'I don't think it's what you *are* that matters. I think it's what you *do*. I think they'd like me just to *be*, and not do anything. That's the trouble.' (p. 168)

This characteristic piece of Pullman philosophy is found in his other novels. So too are the various nineteenth-century references included here, although Princess Aurelia herself has more than a passing resemblance to Lady Diana Spencer, who had died well before this book was published. The attacks on pompous, unfeeling authority, insensitive teachers, vindictive newspapers and bleak orphanages are also at one with an author who is always on the side of the vulnerable and misunderstood. The hope, as always, lies with those humans for whom love and kindness are more important than greed and the trappings of power. Or as the book puts it at the moment when Bob, Joan and their safely returned foster child settle down to a fireside snack: 'The world outside was a difficult place, but toasted cheese and love, and craftsmanship would do to keep them safe.' (p. 175)

Although this story ends happily, there are also moments that have much in common with sections of *His Dark Materials*. The image of an orphaned child up against a heartless organisation is reminiscent of Lyra's plight at some stages. The decision to exterminate the rat boy recalls a similarly pitiless cruelty shown by scientists and their masters towards the children in the hideous camp where Lyra too is briefly imprisoned. But there are also lighter moments, particularly in the many examples printed as if directly from the pages of that imaginary but sadly recognisable newspaper, *The Daily Scourge*. Shown throughout as spiteful, trouble-making and shamelessly inconsistent, at one time going straight from a story urging the death of the rat boy to another celebrating his release, this brilliant exercise in mimicry also makes a more serious point about the dangers of gutter journalism.

Longer Novels

*H*ow To Be Cool (1987) is unlikely to be re-published, if only because what was thought cool at that time would look distinctly old-fashioned now. It describes contemporary Britain threatened by a Coolometer – a device for measuring exactly how cool any individual might be. There is also a sinister National Cool Board, made up of so-called 'cool agents' whose job is to set current trends for the benefit of manufacturers eager to cash in as quickly and effectively as possible. The story ends in farce, with the main child characters organising their own anarchic television show and in so doing making up their minds for themselves about what they con-sider to be truly cool or not. Written at a high pace, this pleasant-enough story never quite achieves take-off. It was however adapted and broadcast in 1988 by Granada Television as a special show on its own.

There is also serious intent beyond the broad humour represented by characters whose trousers sometimes fall down and a trendy headmaster given to using words like 'brill' and 'triff' in an attempt to keep in with his pupils. Pullman clearly detests the modern consumer world of flavour enhancers, artificial colouring and edible chemicals, and goes out of his way to say so. He also insists on a teenager's right to come to his or her own conclusions whatever the commercial pressures that might be brought to bear upon them, in this novel symbolised by the monstrous National Cool Board itself. When the entire physical structure of the universe is threatened by the operation of the Coolometer, Pullman is not just going for dramatic effect. This is one of the many warnings in all his novels about the possible dire consequences of not properly caring for the physical world in which we all live.

The Broken Bridge, written for teenagers before the last story in the Sally Lockhart series, is set in contemporary Britain and is altogether a very different matter. Ginny, its main character, is sixteen and lives with her father. Her mother, she has been told, was a brilliant artist from Haiti who died shortly after Ginny was born. It is from her that Ginny has inherited her dark colour plus a talent for art. But like other Pullman heroines, Ginny is sometimes disturbed by sharp, sudden memories that don't fit in with the stories she has been told about her past. There is also an unsettling visit from a social worker, leading Ginny to wonder whether her beloved father Tony had been holding back on the full truth about her early life. Resigned as an adolescent to being somewhat alone, with the belief that most of the other teenagers around her normally prefer to go out with someone of their own colour, Ginny is then shaken by a series of crises that threaten all her happiness.

The worst of these is the arrival of Robert, a half-brother she had never known about. Now that his mother has died, Robert is coming to live with Ginny and their father, and the first impression he makes is not promising: 'They looked at each other with instant, savage, and mutual hatred.' By this time Ginny has decided that she will never be able to discover more about her origins from her strangely silent father. She throws herself instead into her painting, only to discover that this holds the answer to all the mysteries of her life. After meeting Stuart, an art enthusiast who tell her about Haitian painting, Ginny begins to understand more about herself and in particular her mixed inheritance. The voodoo rites she hears about also seem to be coming to life as well. Voodoo gods, on one tense occasion, actually enter her own head and take temporary possession, giving her a power she finds frightening and gratifying at the same time.

In this mood there is no holding her, and in a final, uneasy alliance with Robert they both seek out their grandparents to get hold of the full story. When it comes, it is told with hatred and prejudice. Ginny's grandmother has unpleasant racist views; she is also very unbalanced. Listening to her, Ginny realises that this is where half of her came from, and she doesn't like it: 'This narrow, prim, cosy, insufferably complacent world of bridge parties and polishing the car and pruning the roses and unfailingly voting Conservative. It was like another planet.'

But she learns enough from this meeting to be able to track down her mother, very far from dead all this time. When they finally meet at an exhibition of her mother's pictures, she is in for another shock. This parent wants nothing to do with her. She also warns her that painting is not the most important thing at all, 'but it'll have to do till we find out what is.' Ginny now sees that it was art that took her mother away from her, because 'art had no conscience; it demanded, it was cruel, it took what it wanted brutally and paid no heed to the consequences.' She also realises that her own skill at art has made her arrogant and unnecessarily stand-offish with other teenagers who might have been more than willing to have had her for a friend. Her story ends as she realises it is important to be sensitive and well disposed to others as well as pushing forward with her own artistic talents. In the final pages, just after she has been asked out on her first proper date, she at last feels at peace both with the community she lives in and with herself.

There are numbers of other sub-plots in this novel, some more convincing than others. Set in Wales, it gives Pullman a chance to show his affection for the Welsh people as well as his familiarity with their language. Although he condemns Ginny's mean, pinched grandmother out of her own mouth, he makes sure that Ginny finally comes to realise that these old people are also desperately unhappy, and that a future meeting where everyone tried to behave normally might still be a possibility.

Ginny also says at one point that 'working was the best thing in the world. Even better than knowing who you were was knowing what you had to do.' She modifies this statement later on, but it still stands as a fair summary of Pullman's belief in getting along, behaving well and always trying to make the best of things. But not knowing truly who you are is such a major concern that it can sometimes stand in the way of everything else. As in other novels by this author, the biggest adventure of all is sometimes a voyage into the past that finishes with a final moment of self-discovery. Although her mother walks away from her, Ginny herself is now stronger, recognising both the British and the Haitian in her background and her art and happy to combine the two. She is also more sympathetic to Robert and more appreciative of her father, once the various malicious rumours about his part in her past have finally been put to rest.

At one point Ginny's best friend Rhiannon complains that 'Sexy people couldn't care less if they're kind or not, but all the kind people'd love to be sexy. The trouble is, you're either one or the other.' By the end of the story, after Ginny has her first date and also feels at one with everyone else, she thinks that Rhiannon might after all have got it wrong. 'Anything was possible, really. Even being kind as well as sexy.' This seems also to be what Pullman himself believes, given that it is a message found in so many of his other books. But he also shows that arriving at this state of positive acceptance can sometimes be hard, and there are many occasions when his main characters face real anguish. Normally for each one of them hope wins over despair, but this is usually shown as a close run victory, with the final outcome unclear until the last few pages.

In his next novel *The Butterfly Tattoo*, formerly known as *The White Mercedes*, the main character ends by losing everything he had hoped for, making this the darkest of Pullman's works to date. It is as if he is warning his readers never to take anything for granted, including the more or less happy endings they might by now have got used to in some of the other novels written for them, including those by Pullman himself.

The Butterfly Tattoo starts with a shocking opening sentence: 'Chris Marshall met the girl he was going to kill on a warm night in early June.' In fact, teenage Chris never for a moment wanted this death to happen, since Jenny, the girl in question, was the love of his life. Meeting her at the Oxford College ball she has gate-crashed, Chris rescues her while she is being chased by some drunken upper-class thugs. Obsessed by her memory, he eventually tracks her down to a nearby squat where she lives with a few other drop-outs. Chris and Jenny go out together and then make love, causing Chris to fall even more deeply for her. But after a series of accidents they are unable to find each other again for some time, however hard they look. When Chris finally locates her, he wrongly believes she is being unfaithful to him. Another misunderstanding leads to her murder by a gunman out to get someone quite different. And it was Chris who led him to where Jenny was hiding out.

Jenny had originally run away from an unhappy home where she was being sexually abused by her father after he became unemployed. But meeting Chris had given her 'a sense she'd never known in waking life and didn't have a name for. In fact, it was goodness; it was the sense of being lapped and bathed in goodness as fresh as the air in spring.' After this promising new start, Jenny begins to see other things differently too. Becoming friends with a nice young mother who was formerly a teacher offers her another step forward. 'Jenny had never thought of teachers as being anything but alien, sullen, hostile failures. The thought of this pretty, pleasant, sensible woman being a teacher made her see all kinds of possibilities for a moment. The world seemed an open and friendly place.'

Chris meanwhile is going through a bad time as he searches for Jenny, having always been more devoted to her than she is to him. Unable any longer to know whom to trust, from his own separated parents to his employer Barry, a small-time crook, he becomes convinced that 'deceit and betrayal were the worst evil, and truthfulness and fidelity the highest good.' He lays into his mother and her new lover for suggesting that the most important thing in life is merely to feel good, 'as if it didn't matter about truth or justice or honour.' Unfortunately, Chris goes on to forget this sound advice for himself. He is persuaded by Carson, the gunman posing as a secret government agent, to break a vital promise he had made which, if he had kept it, would have prevented Jenny's final death.

The arguments Carson uses state that any means are permissible so long as the end results are all right. So instead of continuing to aim for truth and honour, as Chris had always wanted to, he is tricked into agreeing that 'It's no good us fighting clean while these people are fighting dirty, because that would mean we'd lose.' The people Carson refers to here are the imagined Irish terrorists he has dreamed up as a way of getting Chris to betray the whereabouts of the hidden house. Once he knows this location, Carson believes he will find the man he wants to kill. Carson also tells Chris that he has to lose his own innocence if he is ever going to understand what really happens in the world. In just the same way, he argues, it was necessary for Adam and Eve in the Garden of Eden to eat the forbidden fruit from the tree of knowledge in order at last to discover the true nature of both good and evil – shades of *His Dark Materials* still to come.

Chris discovers that losing his own particular innocence at this point by breaking a solemn promise delivers him into what feels like the pit of hell. On the point of suicide after realising that by going against all his basic principles he has in fact delivered Jenny to her death, he still lacks the courage to kill himself. But in a curious twist in the last two pages, living on in shame and despair he finds himself agreeing with the core of what Carson had told him, even though it came from the tongue of a liar.

Carson said that losing innocence is the first step on the road to real knowledge, and Chris now understands. To have any real appreciation of what doing good is, it is also necessary to know the capacity for evil, in oneself as well as in others. And by now Chris has indeed been forced to learn the hard way about the limits of his own nature. 'Unlike anyone around him, he knew precisely how stupid he was, how easily fooled; precisely how much he feared pain; precisely how contemptible he was. Knowledge like that was rare. It put a mark on you. He'd be hard to fool again.'

But there is one more surprise to come. As Jenny lay dying she had written the word 'Dad' on the wall in her own blood. At the inquest held after her death, during a moment when Jenny's father had covered his face with grief, Chris believes that he now understands why she had done this. 'She had loved her father and wanted him there in her last moments; she was calling for help.' Despite the abuse by this same father that she had experienced, Jenny seemed to be demonstrating that the love she once had had for him in better days was still a force powerful enough to forgive the unforgiveable. Chris takes comfort from the idea that even dysfunctional families could offer loving protection in a world that can always be dangerous to the young and innocent.

Some readers may find it hard to follow his reasoning here, given the particular example he chooses of a family fundamentally working against itself. This is a view that Pullman also takes himself, in a letter to me discussing this book. For him, Jenny is still naming the man she most hated. 'Chris, failing to understand it, is interpreting this act of accusation entirely wrongly. Having taken a wrong turning earlier, he is now quite unable to see the truth of things; he's retreated into a false sentimentality, reading things as he thinks they should be rather than as they are.'

Poor Chris, when even his own author takes sides against him! But sentimentality in place of hard-won understanding is something Pullman has no sympathy for. Yet some may feel he is still being rather hard on Chris here, who having gone through a dreadful experience himself could perhaps be excused for not always thinking straight immediately afterwards. And dying individuals may also not always be in a position where they are able to express what they really feel. Pullman himself generously concedes that his own interpretation is only one among many that may be equally valuable. Readers who tackle the book for themselves must make up their own minds about its somewhat ambiguous ending.

These same issues arising from the tension between good and evil, innocence and corruption, attachment and loss are clearly a major concern for Pullman, and are found throughout *His Dark Materials*. As an urban thriller, *The Butterfly Tattoo* is unrelentingly tense and brilliantly successful. The brief love scenes within it come over as moving and convincing. Altogether better plotted than *The Broken Bridge*, it shows Pullman at ease with realism before he had even started writing the longer fantasy novels that were to make him famous.

His Dark Materials

The Stories

Pullman's great trilogy was written over a period of seven years and is around 1,300 pages long. Its cast ranges from scholarly Oxford dons to armoured bears, witches, angels, murderous Spectres and hideous harpies drawn straight from Greek mythology. It can be read at many different levels, from an adventure story to a parable about the essence of human nature and how this has been betrayed. As he puts it himself, it is also a story about what it means 'to be human, to grow up, to suffer, and to learn.' It draws on a wide range of sources, from Ancient Greek myths, the Bible, Dante, John Milton and William Blake to Hollywood films, a Finnish telephone directory and the Superstring theory developed from the study of quantum physics.

Partly arising from a suggestion by Pullman over lunch with his editor David Fickling that his next project might involve a re-writing of Milton's *Paradise Lost*, the trilogy also draws on and develops themes and ideas found in his previous novels. Although it brings numbers of philosophical and scientific ideas into play, it is at base a work of imagination and should always be read as such. For Pullman, the story comes first before everything else, and he strongly believes that it is through stories that humans can best hope to understand both themselves and others. As a writer who has never gone in for too much forward planning, he has also discovered that the story itself as it emerges always knows best, even when it may occasionally seem to be going in an unexpected direction. Sometimes the extra meaning implicit in what he has written, in terms of how it then goes on to inform what happens in the rest of the trilogy, has only become clear to him well after the event.

The basic plot of the trilogy describes how two children, Lyra and Will, manage to overcome forces of oppression to establish a new order based on truth, honesty and love. In so doing, they repeat the original decision of Adam and Eve to seek full understanding and consciousness by eating from the tree of knowledge. But this time the two children, in their own symbolic re-enactment of this original act of defiance, manage to defeat a Church establishment which is still intent on condemning their determined search for freedom as a wicked rebellion.

Involving a whole universe of different human, animal and supernatural players inhabiting a number

13. 'Nearer he drew, and many a walk traversed / Of
stateliest covert, cedar, pine or palm.' (IX 434, 435)
(Source: *Doré's Illustrations for "Paradise Lost"*, Gustave Doré.
Copyright © 1993 by Dover Publications, Inc.)

of parallel worlds, Will and Lyra also have to sort out some personal difficulties with their own parents. They must, too, make a final decision about their growing feelings for each other, when it becomes clear that it will not be possible for them to live together in a world made fresh and new by their joint victory.

The success of this trilogy can be measured in numbers of ways. Sales have been enormous, at one stage outstripping J.K. Rowling's *Harry Potter* books in popularity. *Northern Lights*, the first book of the trilogy (published in America under the title *The Golden Compass*), won both the *Guardian* Fiction prize and the prestigious Carnegie Medal. The third book in the trilogy, *The Amber Spyglass*, was the 2001 Whitbread Book of the Year, the first time this honour has ever been won by a children's book. Three films are planned for the near future, and two plays, both of which will be staged at London's Royal National Theatre from December 2003.

Northern Lights

This story opens with eleven-year-old Lyra Belacqua, accompanied as always by her dæmon Pantalaimon. This is the inseparable, visible spirit that is part of every child in her particular world and can change into any sort of animal. Only later, when an individual turns adult, does the dæmon finally stay in a fixed form for the rest of their life. Lyra and her dæmon are creeping through the darkened main hall of Jordan College, Oxford.

As there is no such college, readers will realise that they are in a world which, as the author says himself, is 'like ours, but different in many ways'. Overhearing a plot by the Master of the College to poison Lord Asriel, the man she believes to be her uncle but who is in fact her father, Lyra prevents him from drinking a fatal draught. After that, she hears Lord Asriel tell colleagues about his discovery of another world running parallel with this one and his determination to explore it. He also talks about Dust, the normally invisible particles that cluster around living beings. The Master of the College has to give up on his plan to stop Lord Asriel's supposedly dangerous enquiries going any further.

In the coming weeks, Lyra becomes aware that some local children have been mysteriously disappearing, including her particular friend Roger, a kitchen boy and the son of a college servant. She also makes the acquaintance of the glamorous Mrs Coulter, without knowing that Mrs Coulter is her mother. Mrs Coulter then plans to take Lyra with her on an exciting journey to the North. But before this happens, the Master of the College, in conditions of the greatest secrecy, presents Lyra with an alethiometer, which he hopes will help protect her from the terrible dangers Lord Asriel seems intent on drawing both himself and his daughter into. Once she has learned to read it, this device will provide her with honest and accurate answers to all the questions she puts to it.

Things soon turn sour with Mrs Coulter, when Lyra learns that she plays an important role in the Church's General Oblation Board. This organisation has been supervising the kidnapping of children from Oxford and elsewhere. The children are then taken far North to Bolvangar, where Lord Asriel is being held captive as well. Lyra runs away to try to free him. She makes contact with John Faa, the leader of the Oxford Gyptians, some tough water gypsies with whom Lyra has had numbers of high-spirited disputes in the past. But everyone is united now in the determination to find the missing children, and Lyra joins an expedition setting out to rescue them. While she is with the Gyptians, she finally learns the truth about who her parents are after talking to John Faa and his aged companion, Farder Coram.

Once the group reaches Lapland, Lyra meets Iorek Byrnison, a talking, armoured bear. He tells them where the lost children are being kept, and how they are being cut away from their dæmons in a hideous operation known as intercision. The Gyptians also meet the American aviator Lee Scoresby, named by Pullman after the actor Lee Van Cleef, who appeared in numbers of films with Clint Eastwood, and William Scoresby, a real-life Arctic explorer. They hire him and his balloon for extra back-up. Lyra becomes friends with Serafina Pekkala too, a witch queen who reveals Lyra's own, particular destiny which is to bring an end to destiny itself. The witch's surname was drawn by Pullman at random from a Finnish phone directory.

As they near their destination, Lyra is kidnapped by a band of Tartars who take her to the special camp which houses the lost children. Scientists hired by the Church Oblation Board are removing the dæmons from all the children who have been rounded up before they can reach adolescence. The Church believes that dæmons help attract Dust to the individual concerned, and that this Dust is synonymous with Original Sin. But Pullman describes Dust instead as the essence of all accumulated human consciousness. It is attracted to adults rather than to children since older people are less innocent and more experienced. If a dæmon is cut away before a child enters puberty, then Dust would no longer be drawn towards the same child once turned adult. And without dæmons everyone becomes much tamer and more manageable, so providing the Church with no trouble when it comes to maintaining and extending its traditional control.

Hiding under an assumed name after she hears

that her mother has arrived at the camp, Lyra meets up again with Roger. Mrs Coulter then rescues her daughter when Lyra is about to be forced to undergo the operation herself. But her mother also wants to get her hands on Lyra's alethiometer. With the help of Iorek the bear plus an army of friendly witches headed by Serafina Pekkala, Lyra escapes with Roger in Lee Scoresby's balloon. This is then attacked by hordes of cliff-ghasts: large, venomous creatures with leather wings and hooked claws. Crashing to earth, Lyra is captured by another tribe of bears who this time turn out to be hostile. Tricking them into allowing Iorek into their midst, Lyra sees her great friend beat his rival Iofur in single combat and so once again take up his rightful leadership of this particular kingdom of the bears.

Lyra then finds Lord Asriel in order to give him the alethiometer she thought he needed, though he can now do without it. In return, he tells her of the great battle that led to the Church condemning Dust as a manifestation of the Original Sin committed when Eve ate the apple from the tree of knowledge in the Garden of Eden. He now wants to travel to other worlds in order to trace the origin of all Dust. But when Lyra wakes up after a night's rest, she finds that her father has departed, taking Roger with him. For in order to travel to another world, her father needs that flash of extra energy generated when a child is separated from his or her dæmon. Roger has been chosen to pay this heavy price. Too late to intervene, Lyra follows him and her father into another world, determined now to find out for herself what Dust is all about.

The Subtle Knife

The narrative starts with Will Parry, a twelve-year-old boy living in modern-day England. Following the disappearance of his explorer-father John on an expedition to the North, Will now has to look after his mentally ill mother. He is taking her to a place of safety after their house has been raided by two sinister men intent on stealing a case of letters and documents belonging to his father. Will foils them, but rightly fears he may have unintentionally killed one of the men.

Running away after leaving his mother in the care of a kind, older friend, he comes across an almost invisible window in the air while walking through the Northern suburbs of Oxford. Passing through it, he finds he is in Cittàgazze, literally the city of the magpies, which acts as a type of crossroads between millions of different worlds. It is an eerie, empty, Italian type of town, only inhabited by children because of the existence of ghost-like Spectres that feed on adults and then leave them as zombies. There he meets Lyra, also lost in this alien world.

Returning together to Will's Oxford, Lyra meets Dr Mary Malone, a scientist working in the University's Dark Matter Research Unit. This dark matter is defined as the so-far undetected stuff that exists between stars and makes gravity work, and which makes up at least ninety percent of the universe. Lyra tells her about Dust, and together the two are able to bring up on a computer screen some elementary particles that seem to have consciousness. Dark matter and Dust turn out to be one and the same thing, or as the angel Balthamos puts it later, 'Dust is only a name for what happens when matter begins to understand itself.'

Lyra loses her alethiometer to Lord Boreal, a smooth-tongued, dishonest collector. He will only give it back if she and Will bring him the very special knife that exists in the other, Italian, world. Returning to Cittàgazze, they finally capture the knife during a fight in the Torre degli Angeli, the Tower of the Angels, which was formerly occupied by the local Guild of Philosophers.

Will is wounded in the process, losing two fingers and bleeding badly. Like many other traditional heroes, he has to pay a harsh price in order to acquire the magical powers he needs. He soon manages to learn how to operate the knife, which is capable of cutting a window into another world at a moment's notice. By now Will has read the letters his father sent home during his final expedition, where he too wrote about the windows that exist between worlds. Will decides that his father may still be alive, and resolves to find him. Back in Oxford, the two children use the knife to cut their way from one world to another, so allowing them access to Lord Boreal's house where they steal back the alethiometer. Lord Boreal is entertaining Mrs Coulter at the time, still anxious to find Lyra.

Meanwhile Lee Scoresby, the aviator, has met up with Stanislaus Grumman, who turns out to be John Parry, Will's father and a self-taught shaman. Grumman too has been investigating Dust, which was why the two hired men, acting on instructions from the Church, were trying to confiscate his papers at the start of the story. He also knows about the knife, though not that it is his own son who now holds it. Grumman desperately wants to find whoever does have it, in order to tell him or her about the vital role it has to play in the future fate of the entire universe.

The soldiers of the Church surround Lee and shoot him dead after a prolonged gun battle. Will at last meets his father, who tells him that the knife is the only weapon capable of killing God himself. But just as they recognise one another after not knowing who they were each talking to, John Parry is slain by the witch he once dared to scorn. Will is then told by two angels to find Lord Asriel, in order to help him in his great fight against the Church authorities. But Lyra meanwhile has disappeared, and Will wonders if he shall ever see her again.

The Amber Spyglass

Lyra is drugged and kept captive by her mother in a secret cave. Mrs Coulter had snatched her daughter away in order to save Lyra from the Church, which wants to kill the child whom it now views as a second Eve. Just as the first Eve was judged to have made trouble by disobeying God's orders, Lyra too is seen as a potential rebel who could, if left alone, re-write human history. Mrs Coulter wants to save her, even though this means opposing the Church for which she had worked so diligently in the past.

Will is still being urged to find Lord Asriel by the two angels, Balthamos and Baruch. They also had taken sides against the ultimate Authority, variously known as 'God, the Creator, the Lord, Yahweh, El, Adonai, the King, the Father, the Almighty'. As Balthamos points out, 'He was never the creator. He was an angel like ourselves – the first angel, true, the most powerful, but he was formed of Dust as we are, and Dust is only a name for what happens when matter begins to understand itself.'

It was this same grim Authority that originally banished Eve after she discovered that he was in fact not the Creator at all. This Authority was later backed by the established Church. His second in command, Metatron, is now out to kill both Will and Lyra. But Will is determined to find Lyra first, as are Iorek the bear, Serafina Pekkala the witch and Lord Roke, Lord Asriel's spy-captain. This gallant gentleman, no taller than six inches, rides on a dragonfly and is the possessor of a lethal pair of poisoned spurs. Father Gomez is also in on the hunt, with a special commission from the Church's Consistorial Court of Discipline to find and eliminate Lyra as soon as possible.

The action then passes to Mary Malone, alone in a world not her own. She meets the strange *mulefa*, peaceful talking animals with horned heads and short trunks who travel around with the aid of two wheel-shaped seed-pods. Their gentle placidity is reminiscent of the Moomin characters invented by the Finnish children's author Tove Jansson, much admired by Pullman as a self-evident genius. But the mulefa are now perpetually raided by cruel, giant bird-shaped creatures known as the *tualapi*. The trees upon which the mulefa depend for their seed-pods are also dying. This is because their world is losing the vital Dust that once allowed it to thrive.

Will locates Lyra, but is nearly taken in by Mrs Coulter's charm. His attempt to rescue her works, although his knife gets broken in the process. Lyra dreams that Roger, her former friend, wants urgently to speak to her, which will necessitate a trip to the land of the dead. After Iorek mends Will's knife, Lyra and Will join a procession of ghosts making their way to the underworld. But when they get to the river dividing the living from the dead, Lyra discovers that she has to leave her beloved dæmon, a part of herself, behind. This is the great sacrifice originally mentioned by the Master of Jordan College, when he revealed that the alethiometer had prophesied that at some stage Lyra would perform an act of terrible betrayal. But she has to do so, agonising and unbearable though it is.

After the crossing she meets Roger, now like her without his dæmon. They encounter some terrifying half-human, half-animal harpies, appointed by the Authority to torment the ghosts of the dead with reminders of all their former wickedness, cruelty and greed. This ghastly process happens to everyone who dies, good or bad alike, because up to now the land of the dead is far from being anything like heaven. It is in fact a place of nothing, 'with no hope of freedom, or joy, or sleep or rest or peace.'

Lyra finds she can get round the harpies by telling them stories that are true at heart. Won over by their enjoyment of these tales, the harpies agree to conduct all future ghosts to the special exit from the underworld that Will and Lyra are planning to make. But this is only on condition that the ghosts involved continue to tell them stories about the lives they once had on earth, true stories about what they've 'seen and heard and loved and known in the world.' Once they leave the land of the dead, they can then happily disappear and in so doing become at one with all other living things on earth. As they approach this moment of final liberation, Will has one last encounter with his father, now a ghost as well.

Mrs Coulter meanwhile has made her way to the President of the Consistorial Court of Discipline, who operates from Geneva. She is imprisoned, but discovers that the President is overseeing the making of a bomb that will kill Lyra once exploded, since it contains a lock of her hair which, with the advanced technology involved, is enough to prove fatal. Mrs Coulter just succeeds in aborting this bomb, and is then rescued, bruised and bleeding, by Lord Asriel. They resolve their differences, each determined to keep Lyra alive at all costs against the different threats facing her.

To this end, Mrs Coulter arranges to meet, and then pretends to seduce, Metatron, The Authority's Regent and the greatest of Lyra's enemies. She tells him she wants to betray her daughter, but this is a ruse to enable Lord Asriel to first ambush and then hurl the wicked angel into an abyss from which there is no return. But he can only do this by sacrificing his own life at the same time, as does Mrs Coulter, having finally admitted to herself that her love for Lyra is now greater than her own wish for survival.

Reunited with Mary Malone, Lyra and Will learn that Dust is leaking from this world because there are now so many windows leading off from it. Will therefore has the duty of closing them, except for one through which the ghosts of the dead can continually pass into the living world before finally disappearing. Father Gomez, Lyra's would-be assassin, is stopped and then killed at the last moment by the angel Balthamos. Lyra and Will find their dæmons once again, and Will is able to see his for the first time.

They realise that they are now in love with each other, but because of the necessity for closing the windows that exist between their two worlds, it will not be possible for them to live together. The option of one staying in the other's world would be impossible, since any prolonged absence from one's own universe inevitably leads to premature old age and death. Instead, Lyra will go to school for the first time in her Oxford while Will must first destroy his knife and then return to the mother who needs him so much. But they will never forget the great love they have for each other, and both are now determined to help build the republic of Heaven on earth, by which they understand the making of the very best, both for themselves and for others, of the life they currently possess.

Will and Lyra

Lyra is a character immediately recognisable from some of Pullman's earlier stories. Mischievous, tough-minded, disrespectful and independent, she is also kind and caring when it most matters. Moving easily between the social classes, she is at home with everyone willing to treat her as a proper person in her own right. No respecter of adult authority, enjoying anarchic mud fights and often in need of a good wash and brush-up, there are moments when, like Thunderbolt in the New Cut Gang stories, she too is close to Richmal Crompton's pre-war child character William.

Spitting plum stones onto the heads of passing scholars or hooting like an owl outside a window where a tutorial is going on are both activities enjoyed by Lyra that William would have been proud to imitate. Cousins, the Master of Jordan's manservant, is at one moment described as 'an old enemy of Lyra's'. This phrase is identical to the descriptions of William's various adult adversaries. Lyra's child friends, and the often ungrammatical English with which they speak to each other, also have something in common with the mode of speech used by William's band of self-styled Outlaws: a gang of children as mischievous as he is himself.

Although Lyra is no orphan, she has had an orphan's upbringing, having been falsely told that her parents had died in an airship accident. Her childhood has been supervised by those living or working in the all-male Jordan College. There is also help from Mrs Lonsdale, a hard-working but unaffectionate housekeeper. This odd background gives Lyra another strong advantage as a storybook heroine. Child heroes who possess loving parents always face a problem in fiction. If they play everything safe, as any properly concerned parent would wish them to, their capacity for adventure is going to be strictly limited. If on the other hand they go in for dangerous exploits, this will mean going against what all good parents would wish for their child. Deliberately running terrible risks is less easy to contemplate with parents who are affectionate, concerned and therefore deserving of trust. But disobeying bad parents, or harsh parent-substitutes, is not a matter for guilt. Accordingly, Lyra stays guilt-free on this issue, given that she does not even know at the start of her story that she has parents who are still living.

When she discovers that they are Mrs Coulter and Lord Asriel, she has even less reason to consider the wishes of such an unpleasant and selfish pair. Having grown up as an orphan, she comes over as someone who has largely invented herself, and who still retains the possibility of reinventing herself once again should the occasion demand. Fictional children possessing caring, hands-on parents can never aspire to the same level of independence which from the start makes Lyra such a potentially interesting as well as attractive character.

She sees her extended family instead as the street urchins, college servants and remote scholars all of whom have taken some loose part in bringing her up. Particular friends like Roger, the Jordan College kitchen boy, play an extra significant part in her life given that she has no other close ties. This helps explain why, in *The Amber Spyglass*, it is so important for Lyra to rescue Roger from the land of the dead. The loyalty she feels towards him is similar to how a sister might react when a beloved brother is killed, partly – as she believes – through her own fault.

At other moments, Lyra feels strongly for a succession of father and mother figures, each one providing the sort of parental love and concern that she has never experienced at first hand. John Faa the Gyptian leader, Iorek Byrnison the armoured bear, Lee Scoresby the aviator, Serafina Pekkala the witch and Mary Malone, the nun-turned-research-scientist, all at some stage perform a role in Lyra's life that would have been more appropriately played by a mother and father. Once again, there are distinct storytelling advantages here. A succession of different, interesting and sometimes bizarre parent-figures is always going to make for more intriguing characters than one pair of ordinarily well-intentioned parents.

As the only girl on John Faa's boat expedition to the North, Lyra soon makes herself busy in the manner of another of Pullman's favourite characters in fiction. This is Tim, the tough small boy in Edward Ardizzone's famous picture book *Little Tim and the Brave Sea Captain* and its various successors. After stowing away on a small boat, Tim is set to work and quickly makes the best of things, even when he seems to be facing certain death. Lyra is also soon on friendly relations with the rest of the crew, and like Tim is allowed to work the ship's steam whistle and help the cook with his plum duff.

This combination of ordinary naughtiness and extreme responsibility under pressure makes her a splendidly well-rounded character, neither oppressively good nor monotonously rebellious. She has those human faults all readers can identify with as well as other virtues that they can freely admire. Nicknamed Silvertongue at one stage, she is also a natural storyteller.

But when Lyra tries to get the better of the harpies by telling them a pack of worthless lies, their indignant screams of 'Liar! Liar!' show her that this policy will never work. The whole episode is a reminder that Lyra's very name, with its overtones of lyre – the instrument of the gods – can also be heard as 'liar' as well. She realises from that moment on that only stories concerned with what she knows to be the truth are going to do. Such stories must draw on her knowledge of what it is really like to be alive, aiming to get everything exactly right as she sees and feels it. In that sense, Lyra stands for the author himself, and his corresponding efforts to get at what he sees as the genuine truth in his imaginative vision of the world, however much this might offend various interested parties along the way.

When interviewed Pullman insists that Lyra is in fact a very ordinary child, and that he had met thousands like her when he was a teacher. As he puts it in the first story of the trilogy, 'She was a coarse and greedy little savage, for the most part.' But he also adds elsewhere that 'The point I am making is that ordinary people are capable of great deeds.' Lyra finally comes through because Pullman believes that all humans have the capacity to be heroic, given the right circumstances. Many would find this an over-optimistic opinion, with Lyra obviously something special by virtue of her outsize courage, superb sense of loyalty and general toughness under fire. But Pullman takes a positive line about human potential wherever it is found. His belief that people can always make the best of their own lives if only they are left alone by religion, or any other authoritarian system of thought, is central to his philosophy.

Although he is the same age, Will is a sadder and more solemn character than Lyra. He has had to shoulder the experience of the loss of his father as well as take responsibility for his mentally ill mother. When others torment her, it is Will who protects her while also trying to cope with his own bruised and angry feelings. Although having already accidentally killed a man is a major worry to him, he still seems drawn to violence. He says at one time to Lyra, 'I got my own things to do in Oxford, and if you give me away, I'll kill you.' As he has previously told her that he is a murderer, she has no reason to disbelieve him.

Without his own visible dæmon for emotional support, Will remains a rather closed personality for most of the trilogy, much in need of more mothering himself. Silent, sometimes moody, but strong and determined when he needs to be, he makes a splendid romantic hero of the old school. It takes his growing feelings for Lyra to give him the confidence to talk about his past unhappiness. When he finally realises that he loves Lyra, he becomes a whole person at last, able to admit to the strong feelings he had up till then kept hidden away. He also by now has the maturity to destroy the knife with which he could have mastered the world.

He does this because he realises that although his own intentions about the possible future uses of the knife are worthy ones, the knife itself has its own plans too, and cannot of itself be trusted. So Will finally breaks it by bringing to mind the one thing it is unable to cut: his love for Lyra. The previous time the knife broke happened when Mrs Coulter filled Will's mind with the image of his much-loved mother. But Will is moving on now in his own maturity, and it is fitting that his love for Lyra now seems to him the most urgent sensation in his life.

He and Lyra both have troubled relationships with their own parents, in one case because there is not enough love and in the other because there may be too much. Resolving their individual psychological needs is something else Will and Lyra have to do on their own, coming out stronger in the end but not before moments of pain. But until they can manage to solve their personal problems they are powerless to see to their most important task, which is nothing less than the saving of the world. The necessity for learning to look both forwards and outwards is another important message in this book, which has little time for those continually trapped in a past that prevents them from enjoying the joys, wonders and duties of the world they are living in at the present.

Will and Lyra as heroes

Fantasies about particular chosen leaders do not always end on a positive note; the mythological leader and saviour King Arthur, for example, dies before his time as part of his destiny. If Pullman's trilogy also ended abruptly in tragedy, it is doubtful whether it would have enjoyed anything like the same success. But although Lyra and Will often suffer, both during their stories and at the moment of their final severance, the whole trilogy is fundamentally about the triumph of good actions over evil ones. This is never a victory that can be taken for granted. As Dr Lanselius says of Lyra, taking his cue from the prophecies made by the witches about her for centuries past, 'she must be free to make mistakes. We must hope that she does not, but we can't guide her.'

As the most important chosen instrument of good, Lyra comes over as an ideal character with whom readers can identify. Sometimes contrary over small details, she is magnificently brave when it really matters. Long realising that she has been picked out to do a special task, however much others believe that she is still ignorant of what her destiny demands of her, she never flinches from this duty. But Lyra has to wait until she finally knows what it is she has to do – which in her case, is to abolish death itself by liberating all those ghosts currently wasting away for ever in a grim underworld.

Will also has his destiny marked out for him, and like Lyra also possesses freedom of choice. As he explains to his father at the end of the trilogy, 'You said I was a warrior. You told me that was my nature, and I shouldn't argue with it. Father, you were wrong. I fought because I had to. I can't choose my nature, but I can choose what I do. And I *will* choose, because now I'm free.'

There is always a problem, however, over freedom of choice with characters who seem to be fulfilling the various prophecies previously made about them. This issue of free will versus destiny is also central to one of Pullman's key influences, Milton's *Paradise Lost*, given that an all-knowing, all-powerful God should surely by definition always have been able to intervene in order to save Adam and Eve from committing their sin in the first place. But Pullman overcomes this problem by making both Will and Lyra such fiercely independent characters that it is impossible to imagine them ever doing anything simply because someone else has told them that they either should or will. What drives them is their sense of what should be, according to their own values and personalities.

This is an important point for both characters, since if they were simply doing what they were always required to do by the greater forces pushing them along they would be little better than robots. But it is not just heroes who must have the power of choice in order to qualify as such. All human beings have to make important choices throughout their lives, and the better they choose, the better it will ultimately be – not just for themselves but also for others. Will and Lyra set an example whereby, whatever the opposition, they insist on making a stand for what they believe to be right. If more people acted in a similar way, the story implies, our own world might be in a much healthier state.

Young people often have a similar fantasy at some stage that they too are extra special, selected by some mysterious force one day to astonish the world. This particular myth of the self frequently lingers on into adulthood, before accumulated experience finally proves to at least most of us that we really are very much like everyone else after all. In Lyra and Will, readers of all ages can identify with young heroes for whom this fantasy is a living reality. No wonder that so many took to them so quickly, with their story stirring up similar fantasies of the type that have always persisted deep in the spirit of all human beings.

It is also interesting that *His Dark Materials* was published at the same time as J.K. Rowling's famous

Harry Potter stories. Both writers, as it happens, had experience of losing a parent when they were still children and both have since admitted to periods of depression in their lives, symbolised by attacks from the Spectres in Pullman's stories and similar assaults by the Dementors in Rowling's novels. Both have had to come to terms with adversity, Rowling as a single mother trying to get by in poverty and Pullman, disappointed after his poor Oxford degree, casting around for an occupation when all he wanted to do was write. It is perhaps no coincidence therefore that both writers have created young characters who have had to battle against the odds before achieving their ends.

Lyra, Will and Harry also come from troubled homes, where there has either been a marked absence of love or else a parent who was not coping. All have been chosen by some unknown force to carry out a great deed that will save the world. All are equal to this task because of their innate courage and moral integrity, and each one possesses an exceptional gift: Harry with his powers of magic, Lyra with her alethiometer and Will with his knife.

They also receive important help from friends but little or nothing from parents or parent-substitutes. Harry is an orphan, Lyra starts by thinking she is one, and Will has never known his father. All are, to this extent, self-created characters, responsible primarily to themselves for want of any parent or parent figure to take responsibility for them. All share the traditional attributes of the fictional lone hero, born in unusual circumstances but with access to extra-ordinary powers. All too are early on linked to a prophecy that marks them out as key figures in the saving of their own society.

Today's fictional heroes are not always so perfect. This is because modern fiction, whether for adults or children, often prefers to go in the direction of psycho-logical realism when describing main characters, avoiding heroics in favour of revealing human flaws as well as strengths. Main characters are often shown as only coming into their own once they have defeated their various personal weaknesses on the way. Others are admired for the way they get the better of severe personal or social disadvantages.

But Lyra, Will and Harry seem to have been born both strong and good. While other children might have become severely disturbed by the sort of child-hood all three endured, they come across as oblivious to every bad influence that might have had a negative effect upon them. The problems they have to defeat come from outside and rarely from their own personalities. The message they carry to readers is that everyone can make it, given the right attitude. Together they signal a return to a simpler fictional world whose heroes nearly always do the right thing.

They also, through their courage, humanity and high sense of morality, represent exemplars of the perpetual human need for undoubted heroes or heroines, if only in the imagination.

Best-selling writers inevitably reflect some of the most popular feelings and fantasies of their own times, and such too could be the case with the creation of Lyra, Will and Harry. In a modern age where biographers, satirists and journalists are eager to cut down anyone who might otherwise seem to be setting a reasonably good or possibly even a heroic example, Lyra, Will and Harry offer a welcome contrast. They are shown throughout to be independent, largely insulated from social influences and very much their own creations. While other characters in their stories are unequal to the mighty task of putting the world to rights, they somehow have the key. Many readers looking at their own world could be forgiven for wishing – at least in their dreams – that similarly wise and brave heroes could one day also sort out some of the most dangerous political and social problems that exist at the moment in real life.

Supporters of genetic engineering have often insisted that they may soon have the techniques to produce babies who are healthy and intelligent as never before. Should this discussion also extend to the possibility of identifying and then adding ideal moral genes to this mixture as well, genetic scientists could well take Lyra, Will and Harry as excellent examples of the sort of humans who could and perhaps should be born as a result.

The whole idea of human perfectibility, whether through genetic engineering or any other process, is of course another fantasy in its own right. Pullman's and Rowling's literary fantasies are of a quite different order, but there may still be some common ground here. Scientists who believe they can one day produce a better type of person and novelists who actually write about such beings are both to an extent reacting to a current dissatisfaction with humans as they actually are and the mess they are making of the world they live in. A general lack of confidence over the future suggests that there is at present little conviction that things will improve unless human beings themselves change for the better. With no evidence that this will ever happen, it is perhaps not surprising that stories about such super-humans, whether fictional or scientific, continue to attract readers of all ages.

There are many other ways in which their stories appeal so powerfully to readers, and in particular to children. All the books in which these characters appear follow a pattern whereby good finally defeats evil in a cosmic battle whose opposing sides are, with some exceptions, clearly drawn. Those readers who have particularly taken to these heroes may be doing so partly because their stories are packed with a type of courage and moral certainty often missing in ordinary human life. Lyra, Will, and Harry do not just represent the best type of character that a new modern hero might one day aspire to be. They also perform valiantly in the service of a moral goodness always clearly visible to them, however difficult it might be to discern in ordinary daily life well away from the world of storytelling.

Science and Religion

Knowing your enemy: Lyra and Will versus the Church

Early on the alethiometer reveals that Lyra is going to play an important part in a major battle. This has started as a dispute between the Holy Church and her own father over the possible existence of other worlds beyond the present one and the conventional Christian view of one other spiritual world made up of heaven and hell. Later on this turns into a fight to the death between those who support further enslavement by the evil Church forces versus those who wanted final liberation from the curse humankind has laboured under ever since the first condemnation of Eve.

This story can also be read as a fable, with Lyra and Will standing in for Adam and Eve. The suggestion is that our own cultural history might have developed along far healthier lines had the story of the Garden of Eden been interpreted in the first place with Eve the heroine rather than the villain of the piece. Far from an act of tragic disobedience, Pullman clearly believes that her decision to eat the apple from the tree of knowledge was the right thing to do.

All the disgrace visited upon this action since stems in his view from the Church's determination to keep everyone in a state of continual guilt and fear. Congregations brought up to feel like this are then all the more willing to turn towards an organised religion that promises redemption for the first great, human sin that Pullman believes should never have been described in that way. Now, in a re-run of this famous story, Lyra and Will also disobey the teachings of the Church, but are seen by their supporters to have done the right thing, not just for themselves but for everyone else as well.

Lyra starts out as a child in the trilogy, but finishes with the experience of a first, passionate love affair. As Mrs Coulter puts it to the evil President of the Consistorial Court, 'My daughter is now twelve years old. Very soon she will approach the cusp of adolescence, and then it will be too late for any of us to prevent the catastrophe; nature and opportunity will come together like spark and tinder.'

As so often, Mrs Coulter is playing a double game here, and next moment she turns against the Church, describing the whole court as 'a body of men with a feverish obsession with sexuality, men with dirty fingernails, reeking of ancient sweat, men whose furtive imaginations would crawl over [Lyra's] body like cockroaches'. But there is no doubt that the court sees Lyra's progress towards taking up a positive attitude about her own sexuality as a severe threat. Should she, like Eve before her, also give way to what the Church defines as temptation but which Lyra would experience as love without guilt, this will surely ruin the authority of the whole ecclesiastical establishment. That is why its president, Father MacPhail, proposes to send out someone to kill her.

Once again there is a strong parallel with the story of Adam and Eve. Yet Pullman suggests that the overwhelming sense of shame described in the Bible after the couple became aware of their naked sexuality for the first time, far from being a natural outcome, was actually imposed upon them by the grim-faced Authority. This action then allowed him a perfect method of control over them and subsequently everyone else. Since all humans coming after Adam and Eve would inevitably develop sexual awareness, being taught to feel bad about such feelings allowed the Authority, now naming himself as God, a perfect method of control ever after. Having imposed a seal of shame on all believers, the Church could then set itself up as the only institution capable of bestowing forgiveness for a state of consciousness that in fact never needed to be excused or forgiven in the first place.

But if Lyra, as a modern Eve, discovers that her first consciousness of sexuality is a joyful and loving process, then the former power of the Church to impose guilt and fear in this area could be lost for ever. Exactly how Lyra's example would filter through to everyone else is never made clear. But everyone in the trilogy knows how important Lyra is and how long her presence has been prophesied. The ultimate positive effect she will have on her own society if she wins through must simply be taken for granted.

Pullman's attack on Christianity takes off in other directions. He is not against the idea of one great force in the universe, of the type that makes the northern lights glow and may be pushing the hands of the alethiometer at the same time. But he hates all the attempts by human agencies to first claim this force for themselves and then use it for evil purposes. God, or the Authority, is simply in this trilogy the first angel to be 'condensed out of Dust'. He told all the angels that came after him that he was their creator, but this was not true.

At the end of the trilogy, this figure is revealed to Mrs Coulter as nothing more than an anguished, aged being, 'of terrifying decrepitude, of a face sunken in wrinkles, of trembling hands and a mumbling mouth and rheumy eyes'. Demented and powerless, he finally dissolves in the wind after Lyra and Will help him out of his crystal litter. He does so with 'a sigh of the most profound and exhausted relief'. His Regent, Metatron, who had long been running things, is the Biblical figure Enoch, a direct descendant of Adam. He too is anxious for power and ruthless about how he gets it, and is well served on earth by the Church, which uses the original lies of the Authority to back up its own claims for power over other fellow humans.

This ultra-negative view of Christianity and the Church could seem strange at a time now when, at least in the Western world, religious belief is generally on the wane. But Pullman is having nothing of this. In his lecture on the republic of Heaven, given in March 2000, he writes 'of all the dangers that threaten us at the beginning of the third millennium – the degradation of the environment, the increasingly undemocratic power of the great corporations, the continuing threats to peace in regions full of decaying nuclear weapons, and so on – one of the biggest dangers of all comes from fundamentalist religion.' He goes on to pick out in particular the threat posed at the time by Christian conservatives in the USA and the Taliban in Afghanistan.

One of the arguments for any organised religion has always been that humans need a fixed code of

14. A watercolour painting from William Blake's *Book of Urizen*: 'The Immortal endur'd his chains, / Tho' bound in a deadly sleep.' Blake has been a particular hero and influence on Pullman. (*The Book of Urizen* (1794), plate 22, copy G, c. 1815. Reproduced by permission of the Library of Congress.)

125

conduct without which they may be too weak to conduct their lives for the best. Pullman rejects this case on both counts. He does not think that the code of conduct suggested by Christianity is either good or humane, and he believes that humans have it within themselves to live happy, fulfilled lives without encouragement or threats from religion. But as he has admitted himself, 'There is a depressing human tendency to say "We know the truth and we're going to kill you because you don't believe in it."' Why so many human beings should have lent themselves to attitudes like this both in the past and present, and what this means for Pullman's more hopeful view about humanity, is a matter his novels have yet to come to terms with.

As far as Western Europe is concerned, Pullman's reasons for his passionate dislike of Christianity in the trilogy sometimes belong to the remote past. He twice mentions the fact that John Calvin, the seventeenth-century Protestant Reformer based in Geneva, occasionally ordered the deaths of children he believed to be heretics. Elsewhere, the witch Serafina Pekkala warns her sisters that there are modern churches that cut children's sexual organs 'with knives so that they shan't feel'. But if this is a reference to female genital mutilation, this is something that Christian forces in Africa have long been condemning. If the target is the ritual circumcision of boys, it seems harsh to blame this practice on the influence of religion alone.

Pullman gives a clue to what he is getting at here when Lord Asriel lectures Lyra about the Church's tradition of cutting children:

> Do you know what the word *castration* means? It means removing the sexual organs of a boy so that he never develops the characteristics of a man. A *castrato* keeps his high treble voice all his life, which is why the Church allowed it: so useful in Church music. Some *castrati* became great singers, wonderful artists. Many just became fat spoiled half-men. Some died from the effects of the operation. But the Church wouldn't flinch at the idea of a little *cut*, you see.'

This loathsome practice is not found in any Christian religion today, and was once widespread in many quite different cultures. So once again, it seems hard to blame it on Christianity alone. The various priest characters in the trilogy, whether they enjoy vodka too much, watch over acts of torture or set out to commit murder, also come over as uniformly nasty. Like the caricatures found in the atheistic propaganda put over in pre-war Soviet Russia, these characters suggest that a good clergyman or nun has never existed. This is clearly unfair, as is the suggestion in the trilogy that the Church is only concerned with its own cruel and cynical survival, and is happy to kidnap, torture and murder to that end.

Pullman believes that 'Every single religion that has a monotheistic god ends up by persecuting other people and killing them because they don't accept him. Wherever you look in history you find that. It's still going on.' But since he knows the Christian religion best, this is where he pitches his main attack. For him, Christianity is a powerful and convincing mistake that has adversely shaped Western culture ever since it was first adopted. In this view, the Christian concept of the Kingdom of Heaven has always been an authoritarian attempt to impose negative values on populations, backed up by the whole weight of a self-serving Church hierarchy.

The end result has been an inevitable persecution of those who oppose this system of belief. Such persecution is certainly less obvious now than it has been in the past. But in terms of the trilogy, Lyra's world of Brytain is different in many ways from Will's up-to-date version of Britain today. If the powers of the Church in Lyra's life have developed in new and horrible directions this, in Pullman's view, is because the seeds of this type of religious tyranny have always been implicit in Christianity anyway. While such tyranny is relatively restrained in Will's world, it is running out of control in Lyra's Brytain, just as it sometimes did in our own past.

What Pullman argues for instead is the reverse ideal of a *republic* of Heaven, inhabited by people who have been brought up to value both themselves and others. In this scenario, the guilt and shame about sex encouraged by the Bible would be replaced by an honest admission of the joys and pleasures of the body. Instead of turning to priests and the Bible for advice, people instead should learn to trust their own instincts to do the right thing. The aim should always be to live harmoniously with themselves and with each other in an environment that is also loved and protected. Far from condemning Eve for eating from the tree of knowledge, Pullman believes that she should be seen as heroic in her determination to find out things for herself – the basis for all true education.

As for the powers of the Church as they appear in his trilogy, it is clear that Pullman is not only aiming at oppressive religion in his description of the various forces of darkness threatening to take over every world wherever they exist. He is also attacking all authoritarian systems of thought, religious or otherwise, that set out to enslave their followers under the guise of caring for them. As John Parry puts it to his son, 'Every little increase in human freedom has been fought over ferociously between those who want us to know more and be wiser and stronger, and those who want us to obey and be humble and submit.'

Some would argue that there are times in history as well as in the contemporary world when this apparently clear division between good and bad is not as easy to make out. But in broad terms at least, this overall view enables Pullman to attack many other villains in addition to oppressive religion in his trilogy. The cruelty inflicted on the kidnapped children when their dæmons are cut away is more reminiscent of some of the abominable experiments carried out in Nazi concentration camps than anything to do with the modern Church as such.

The spiritual starvation and environmental degradation that so often go together in modern dictatorships are also a twin feature in the various descriptions of lost, cowed societies found in the trilogy. Lyra does not just stand for spiritual freedom; she also represents the physical and social freedom that should be the aim of any truly civilised country for its citizens, young or old. This is not an argument for anarchy, given that Pullman also provides plenty of examples where individuals act with a just authority that deserves to be obeyed, from Iorek the bear to Dame Hannah, the wise headteacher who takes on Lyra as her pupil at the end of the trilogy. But such authority must be earned rather than assumed, and it should always act with a strong sense of responsibility.

Parallel worlds

Lyra and Will live in parallel worlds, res[...] other in some ways but different in ot[...] course of their travels, they enter other wo[...] [...]en. This may seem a strange direction to take for a writer so intent on the idea of making the best of the here and now in his fiction. Yet there are good reasons for this plot device. Pullman takes his cue here from modern quantum theory, which replaces former truths once held to be standard with the idea of uncertainty as a built-in factor to all science.

This has led distinguished physicists such as David Deutsch to claim that the results of certain 'double slit' experiments with light constitute evidence for the existence of parallel worlds. This claim has been disputed, but the main argument, once unthinkable where orthodox scientific reasoning is concerned, still has its followers. The Palmerian Professor at Jordan College refers it to when he mentions 'the Barnard-Stokes business' to Lord Asriel at the start of *Northern Lights*. Later on, the Master of Jordan explains to the librarian how these two daring theologians had postulated 'the existence of numerous other worlds like this one, neither heaven nor hell, but material and sinful.'

The basic premise about the possible existence of parallel universes arises from what might happen ould one particular action have two possible results at the same moment. Let Pullman explain the main idea behind this for himself, talking through the pursed lips of Lord Asriel:

> Take the example of tossing a coin: it can come down heads or tails, and we don't know before it lands which way it's going to fall. If it comes down heads, that means that the possibility of its coming down tails has collapsed. Until that moment the two possibilities were equal.
>
> But on another world, it does come down tails. And when that happens, the two worlds split apart. I'm using the example of tossing a coin to make it clearer. In fact, these possibility-collapses happen at the level of elementary particles, but they happen in just the same way: one moment several things are possible, the next moment only one happens, and the rest don't exist. Except that other worlds have sprung into being, on which they *did* happen.

Pullman puts this idea of other worlds to maximum use in his trilogy, showing readers how each of the societies that he describes has gone on to grow in its own particular style. The same is true of individual development. Will and Lyra reflect while sitting together on a moss-covered rock on 'how many tiny chances had conspired to bring them to this place.

Each of those chances might have gone a different way'. The overall message is that because nothing that happens is ever inevitable, it is up to the people that live in whichever world – including our own – always to make the best of the various opportunities that come their way.

At a plot level, parallel universes also have advantages, allowing Pullman to use his gift for describing other worlds that are a fascinating mixture of the strange and the familiar. Some of these details of daily life in other worlds are drawn not just from the present but also from the nineteenth century, such as the naphtha lights and zeppelins that crop up throughout the trilogy. Others are entirely imaginary, like the alethiometer, a device for reading the future taking its name from *aletheia*, the Greek word for truth, or the various dæmons that accompany people in Lyra's world. In all cases, the effect is to keep the reader in a state of imaginative wonder – for Pullman, one of the principal aims of all fiction.

What is Dust?

Pullman never actually states who or what he thinks does actually run the universe, and for good reason. To do so would be to run into exactly the same trap that has snared everyone else attempting to narrow down and specify a power that he believes remains impossible to understand, however clearly it is sometimes felt. At one moment Serafina Pekkala tells Lee Scoresby of Lyra that 'it seems that the fates are using her as a messenger to take [the alethiometer] to her father'. Later on Jotham Santelia, Professor of Cosmology, assures Lyra that 'The stars are alive, child. Did you know that? Everything out there is alive, and there are grand purposes abroad! The universe is full of *intentions*, you know. Everything happens for a purpose.'

It is a short step from this position to move on to the idea that the elementary particles that make up life may themselves also possess consciousness, just as they do in the Dust that plays such an important part in all three stories. Pullman takes his own particular use of this word straight from a verse in the Bible. When God is cursing Adam for having eaten the forbidden fruit, he tells him 'For dust thou art, and unto dust shalt thou return.'

As Lord Asriel explains to Lyra, some scholars believe this should actually be translated as 'thou shalt be subject to dust'. But for Pullman, Dust has many different meanings. He defines it variously throughout the trilogy as original sin, the form of thoughts not yet born, dark matter, shadow-particles, particles of consciousness and even as rebel angels. This cosmic Dust is distributed throughout space and is at one with the universe itself. Death is described as a joyful process of re-integration with Dust rather than with any Christian idea of God. This belief is not far from the eighteenth-century idea of pantheism, whereby God is seen as everything and everything is seen as God.

Pantheism is in fact a very ancient belief, far older than Christianity, and forms the basis for many other world religions still in existence today. At its heart is a reverence for the whole universe as well as for the native earth, seen as something sacred. Supernatural gods play no part in this religion. Animal as well as human rights are respected, and there is a commitment never to harm the natural environment. Humans themselves are held to be made of the same matter as the universe, and only in this life do they have the chance to witness this earthly paradise face to face. When they die, they are reunited with nature by being re-absorbed into it. But should they destroy nature, they then risk creating a hell on earth for all species as well as for themselves.

Pullman's notion of Dust may therefore also have links with a particular mystical-ecological approach to the earth. In this view the world – like Dust – has always been a living organism with its own needs and feelings. The Greeks recognised this by giving the earth its own individual name of Gaia, the Greek name for the Goddess who was the original earth-mother. Humankind that so freely pollutes the world continues to neglect this mighty living organism at its own extreme peril.

His Dark Materials is packed with examples of environmental devastation, running hand in hand with descriptions of accompanying human cruelty, neglect and intolerance. For Pullman, bad behaviour towards other humans is inseparable from behaving badly towards the living environment. In both cases, violence is shattering what should be a natural harmony and still could be, if only humans learned how to act in ways where 'responsibility and delight can co-exist'. In this, they could well afford to follow the example of the gentle, inoffensive mulefa, who work *with*, rather than against, their environment. By using giant seed-pods as wheels to help them travel, they also bring these same pods to a state where they finally crack after so much pounding along hard roads. After that, it is possible for the mulefa to extract the seeds which are then tended carefully as they grow into new plants.

Dust may also be linked to Superstring Theory found in the discussion of quantum physics today. Sometimes also known as the Theory of Everything, this states that at the most microscopic level every-thing in the universe is made up of loops of vibrating strings. An object such as an apple, and a force such as radiation, can in this theory both be broken down into atoms, which can then be further broken down into electrons and quarks. These in turn can finally be reduced to tiny, vibrating loops of string.

This essential indivisibility of matter and energy could help explain how Dust has consciousness as well as an only barely visible physical shape. As Dr Malone discovers, it made its presence felt in human evolution partly in order to extract vengeance. This was for the betrayal of humanity that occurred when the rebel angels lost the great battle that once raged in heaven. These angels were also composed of Dust.

At other times this precious shadow-matter can only be approached obliquely. When Lyra turns to the alethiometer, or Will makes use of his knife, it is important that they stay in a relaxed, totally open and receptive state of mind, putting their own immediate thoughts to one side. Yet if humans can never confront Dust directly, they can still become conscious of examples of its essential truth so long as they remember to look out for them. The better any of us live, Pullman says, the more likely that we too might experience the type of positive joy that also drives the entire world. Cruelty, greed and selfishness, on the other hand, only obscure what is good and true. When these negative impulses become linked to evil political or religious movements, the results can be disastrous. Dust, of itself, has no power to shape human lives. Only we can do that; but by doing the best we can we will, in Pullman's view, then be working in the true spirit of this special Dust rather than against it.

This is not to say that Dust in itself, when we finally return to it, offers a better alternative to life on earth. When Serafina Pekkala watches the gleaming angels flying away, she feels nothing but compassion for these magnificent beings composed only of light and Dust. 'How much they must miss, never to feel the earth beneath their feet, or the wind in their hair, or the tingle of the starlight on their bare skin!'

Later on, Mrs Coulter makes the important discovery about angels that 'lacking flesh, they coveted it and longed for contact with it'. For Pullman, it is still best to be human, enjoying all the legitimate pleasures of the body that we have been blessed with but which religion in the past has sometimes condemned so cruelly. As Will explains to Lyra, 'Angels wish they had bodies. They told me that angels can't understand why *we* don't enjoy the world more. It would be [a] sort of ecstasy for them to have our flesh and our senses.'

He is not simply referring to sexuality here. Pullman is an enthusiast for all types of physical joy, there to be relished without the shame and guilt that religion has sometimes tried to attach to any sort of sensual enjoyment in life. A good example of what he believes occurs at the moment when Mary

Malone feels she is somehow being carried away from her own body and desperately attempts to fight back:

> She flung a mental lifeline to that physical self, and tried to recall the feeling of being in it: all the sensations that made up being alive. ... The taste of bacon and eggs. The triumphant strain in her muscles as she pulled herself up a rockface. The delicate dancing of her fingers on a computer keyboard. The smell of roasting coffee. The warmth of her bed on a winter night.'

Mary survives this episode; Pullman makes it clear that her survival is supremely well worth it, given the capacity she and so many other humans beings have to find such delight in comparatively simple pleasures. But those children cut away from their dæmons before reaching adolescence will never get to experience such strong feelings in any areas of their lives. Mrs Coulter tries to explain the positive side of this whole, cruel practice of intercision to an unconvinced Lyra. 'All that happens is a little cut, and then everything's peaceful. For ever! You see, your dæmon's a wonderful friend and companion when you're young, but at the age we call puberty ... dæmons bring all sorts of troublesome thoughts and feelings, and that's what lets Dust in.'

Losing a dæmon, therefore, is akin to losing an individual's adult soul. Without it, there can be no contact with that vital Dust that is also synonymous with energy, consciousness and freedom of thought. Like the victims of the Spectres, those without dæmons become 'indifferent [and] dead in life'. But with their own dæmons and therefore open to attracting Dust as adults, individuals are able to become fully formed human beings, conscious of their own potential and able to make informed decisions about the rest of their lives.

So who or what is in ultimate control of everything? What force, for example, both powers and informs the alethiometer? Who exactly picked out Lyra for her great task of saving the world, and who originally prophesied that it would be a girl who would be the chosen saviour? Pullman offers no clear answers here, nor does he wish to. Instead, he quotes with approval the poet Keats' belief that it is only possible to write a good poem when a man is 'capable of being in uncertainties, mysteries, doubts, without any irritable reaching after fact and reason'. So while it is soon clear how much Pullman disapproves of systems of thought such as organised religion that attempt to explain and account for everything within the world and the spirit, his own belief system is more intuitive than worked out to the last letter.

Dæmons

Lyra's dæmon is named Pantalaimon, which means 'all merciful' in Greek. The word 'dæmon' also derives from the Greek, with Socrates at one stage talking about his own *daimon*, which in his terms was a cross between a conscience and a guardian angel. Always addressed as Pan, Lyra's dæmon is a visible personal soul or spirit, able to take on any animal form. Everyone in Lyra's world has his or her own dæmon, whose shape only becomes constant once an individual has grown beyond childhood into late adolescence. Such dæmons act variously as confidants, advisers, spies, look-outs, defenders, occasional scolds, best-loved intimates and, most especially, the voice of conscience when the going gets tough.

They are particularly important in this story where Lyra is concerned. As a child with an absent, neglectful mother and a father who is almost as bad, Lyra has the type of childhood that in normal circumstances would be described as severely deprived. Although the tutors at Jordan College take an absent-minded interest in her, there is no one who clearly loves her and whom she can love in return – except, of course, for her dæmon.

Pan therefore has a vital role in this story. Like nearly all dæmons, he is of the opposite sex to his human counterpart. As such, he corresponds to the psychologist Carl Jung's idea that all humans have a craving for an other half, also of the opposite sex which, if we could reunite with it, would then mean that we could at last become truly whole individuals. This concept is described in Jungian terms as the life-long search for the *anima*, where men are concerned, and the *animus* in the case of women. But because we can never be joined up to our missing male or female counterparts, Jung believes we must always go through life with the feeling that there is something important missing within us.

Lyra has no such problems, since her dæmon already gives her all the love and support she needs. This is vital for the plot, since it would otherwise be difficult even to start believing that a ten-year-old girl on her own could be equal to any of the acts of daring and courage that Lyra manages to carry off through-out this story. In real life, a child as deprived as she is might instead have major and sometimes disabling psychological problems to deal with long before getting to the fearful adventures she confronts in this story.

But with her own dæmon as constant support and always ready with a friendly word or understanding look, Lyra can take on any of the tasks at hand. Readers, in their turn, are offered an exceptionally pleasing fantasy of the type that has always been popular in children's fiction, with its long tradition of describing heroes who also possess ideal companions. From the story of Dick Whittington's cat to modern classics like Clive King's *Stig of the Dump* and Raymond Briggs's *The Snowman*, the idea of the main character blessed with a close and beloved friend has been a constant theme both in children's and adult literature. Hamlet has always needed his Horatio, Don Quixote could never manage without his patient servant Sancho Panza, and Sherlock Holmes would not have had half as good a time without his great friend Dr Watson.

But more recently in teenage fiction, there seems to have been less emphasis upon the role of the special friend, once such a familiar figure in any story. There are several reasons why fiction may be following contemporary trends in this respect. Fewer pupils now go to the same-sex boarding schools that once provided a natural background for strong and special friendships. Instead, teenagers now expect to develop romantically-oriented relationships with the opposite sex far earlier than was once the case, leaving less time for more ordinary, less intense same-sex friendships. The time that proper friendship requires in order to get established is more limited now in other ways, with ever-more-demanding schoolwork during term and holiday jobs in the vacations. Spending a lot of time away from home, with or without friends, is also less popular with parents now, anxious that something may happen to their children when they are not there.

Best friends still exist in teenage books, but there don't seem to be quite so many these days, and those that there are can sometimes turn into a worst enemy. This happens in Anne Fine's memorable novel *The Tulip Touch*, and there are other stories where friendship causes as many problems as it once seemed to solve. Against this background, the idea of a personal dæmon offers all the consolations of the closest and most intense friendship without any of the possible disadvantages. The British psychotherapist Donald Winnicott once wrote that every individual has the need to create what he called a 'caretaker self.' This is that internal voice that tries to cheer up someone particularly when he or she is down, in general acting as a sympathetic and reassuring friend at all times.

In this sense, dæmons too can surely claim to be caretaker selves of a different order. Always on the side of their human counterpart, they can actually be seen and heard as well as felt. Will can't wait to see his dæmon who has hitherto always been invisible to him. When she finally flies down, 'he felt his heart tighten and release in a way he never forgot'. So to the great love between Will and Lyra that serves as the final climax of the trilogy can also be added the equally profound love they have for their respective dæmons. Both of these loving and intimate relationships – to each other as well as to their dæmons – represent an ideal to which humans have constantly aspired.

Realistic novels for young readers have always stressed the pain experienced by children suffering from adverse social or psychological conditions, should such characters be part of the general plot. After finishing such a book, readers as well as feeling entertained by a good story may also now be extra alert to the various signs of mental or physical stress in children who are going through a particularly difficult time in real life. But fantasy stories, including this trilogy, often have a quite different sort of agenda. They may be more concerned with extending the imaginative world into the realms of the truly extra-ordinary, making use of main characters able to survive everything thrown at them precisely because they do not have the weaknesses and problems common in real life.

But there may still be a problem of credibility here, even in a fantasy story, when it comes to making such bold adventurers believable at the same time. So giving Lyra the additional backing of her own personalised dæmon is one brilliant way of effectively winning readers over to the idea that she really could always behave in the courageous and independent way that she does. It also enables Pullman to turn what would normally be private thoughts into an ongoing dialogue, given that Lyra and her dæmon constantly talk to and argue with each other throughout their story. This is particularly true in moments of stress when it comes to deciding what to do next.

Lord Asriel and Mrs Coulter

Lord Asriel is Lyra's unloving, superior and short-tempered father. Is he on the side of good and Dust or is he simply playing his own selfish game? Like Satan in Milton's *Paradise Lost*, he is a mixture of both good and bad. His mighty ambition is to destroy God himself, just as Milton's Satan wants to wage a war in order to regain heaven after his expulsion for rebelling against God. But after more thought, Satan decides to investigate new worlds instead, just as Lord Asriel does. Like Satan, by building a bridge to another world Lord Asriel risks upsetting the natural order, and in so doing may have been instrumental in introducing the plague of Spectres unleashed on the world. It is for this type of reason that the otherwise kindly Master of Jordan College tries to poison him early on, conscious that if his bold scientific investigations into other worlds were allowed to continue they could eventually bring disaster for all in their wake.

Although Milton describes Satan as evil and malicious, readers often find something heroic in the depiction of Satan, and the terrible energy that goes into his quest for power and revenge. As William Blake put it, 'The reason Milton wrote in fetters when he wrote of angels and heaven, and at liberty when he wrote of devils and hell, is that he was a true poet and of the devil's party without knowing it.' Lord Asriel too is a more vivid, colourful figure than some of the more anodyne angel characters that crop up in Pullman's books. When he appears, things happen, however unpleasantly he may behave in the process.

Lord Asriel finally dies in his determination to save his daughter Lyra, a second Eve. He is also determined to protect Dust from its many enemies, and fights bravely in the various pitched battles that result from doing this. So on this basis, both Satan and Lord Asriel could be seen to be on the side of essential human freedom. While Satan battled in vain against what Pullman sees as a jealous and restrictive God, Lord Asriel takes up the fight against the evils of organised religion that have in this account plagued humankind ever since.

Milton's Satan also suffered from a sinful pride that constantly led him to make bad decisions. The same too is true of Lord Asriel. Cold and rejecting towards his daughter, he is willing to sacrifice the life of a child in order to further his attempts to travel to another world. He revels in his scientific power not just for what it can achieve but also for its own sake. When he boasts to Mrs Coulter that 'You and I could take the universe to pieces and put it together again', there seems little doubt that he is beginning to think that he is God himself. As his servant Thorold confides to Serafina Pekkala, 'his ambition is limitless. He dares to do what men and women don't even dare to think.'

Thorold goes on to say that this makes him either 'mad, wicked, deranged' or else a man like no other, exceeding even angels in his determination and ultimate capacity to put right an ancient wrong. But his fierce pride, so important in motivating him for his great task, also blinds him to the value of others, in particular his own daughter. Only in the closing pages of the trilogy does he realise that her life is actually more important than his own. By this time he has understood that his determination to live in other worlds has been fundamentally mistaken. As the ghost of Will's father John Parry observes, 'we have to build the republic of heaven where we are, because for us there is no elsewhere.'

This is because a dæmon can only live its full life in the world in which it is born. In the same way, Pullman suggests, we too must always make the best of where we are. But Lord Asriel realises almost too late that his loyalties must stay with his own universe, and in particular with his daughter. A deeply flawed hero, he always runs the risk of turning into just the type of bullying authority he had made it his life's work to destroy. Sacrificing his life to save Lyra is not just a noble act; it is also a final admission that he is ultimately expendable, and to that extent a servant of fate rather than, as he once believed, its potential master.

Mrs Coulter, the mother of his daughter, is an even less attractive character. A faithful servant of the Church, she is party to numbers of its worst acts and joins in enthusiastically herself with the torturing to death of a young witch. Manipulative, scheming, insincere and ruthless, she is the mother from hell. Flattering Lyra with soft words and shows of affection at one moment, acting like a cruel bully the next, she is never to be trusted. Unlike Lord Asriel, she takes no major role in the great battle between good and evil. Instead she always chooses to play her own game, seeking out every advantage first for herself and then, if it seems convenient, for her employers too.

Mrs Coulter uses her great beauty to maximum effect, charming not just Metatron but also Will when he is on his mission to rescue Lyra. Sensing his guilt about having been away from his own vulnerable mother for so long, she works on him to the extent that he ends by breaking his precious knife under the emotional strain. But as everyone who temporarily falls for her soon discovers, feminine allure is a false friend unless also accompanied by love and kindness. Like the wicked Queen in *Snow White*, Mrs Coulter is additionally frightening simply because she comes over as so beautiful as well.

Discovering that appearances are often deceptive is a lesson every child has to learn at some stage. Should the person concerned also be their own parent, this lesson can prove a particularly bitter experience. Although most children are more fortunate than Lyra with their own mothers, Mrs Coulter's presence in the story is a powerful reminder that evil can be just as bad even when it is hiding behind not just a pretty but also a familiar face.

So what are readers to make of Mrs Coulter's final discovery that she does love Lyra after all, even to the extent of giving up her own life so that her daughter might live? There is no doubt of her sincerity here, but this is not because she now genuinely regrets all the other evil things she has done in her life, even though she is fully aware of how low she has descended over the years. Instead, it seems that her maternal instinct, however deeply suppressed before, has at last come to the surface in a way that won't be denied. Having been loved by many other people in vain, she at last has the experience of loving someone back in return. So while Lord Asriel stands for intellectual ambition gone mad, Mrs Coulter symbolises the emotional world of strong, distorted feelings, where self-love battles against an underlying need to provide maternal care when it is most needed.

Both characters also serve as reminders that any final division of characters into good and evil is never easy and often impossible. Just as Milton's Satan has his darkly attractive side, so too do Lord Asriel and Mrs Coulter refuse to behave either entirely admirably or disgracefully. As Pullman has written elsewhere, 'No-one is purely good or purely evil … I would much rather we thought in terms of good actions, bad actions.'

In his other novels he has also shown that conventionally bad characters can still sometimes get the better of an argument. But despite these qualifications, it is usually clear where Pullman's sympathies lie. This is particularly so with his minor characters, where there is less time to spell out any of their possible accompanying moral complexities. As in the Victorian melodrama and children's adventure comics he so loves, there is no shortage of truly villainous beings in his books, particularly at those moments when it is time for another twist in the plot in order to bring about yet more excitement and suspense.

Influences and Comparisons

John Milton

John Milton's epic poem *Paradise Lost*, written between 1658 and 1663, is one of the greatest literary creations of all time. Drawn from the Old Testament, it sets out to 'justify the ways of God to Men' by retelling the story of how Adam and Eve came to be expelled from the paradise of living in the Garden of Eden. It starts with Satan surrounded by fallen angels who, like him, have been expelled from Heaven to live in the Abyss of Hell. Nothing daunted, he resolves to build the rival kingdom of Pandemonium. But rather than risk another war against God, Satan decides to get back at his hated rival in a more subtle way.

Escaping from Hell, accompanied by his daughter Sin and their joint son Death, Satan sets out to wreck God's plans for His newly created earth. Coming across Adam and Eve living a perfect life untouched by any flaws, guilt or death, Satan starts tempting Eve in dreams to do the only thing she and Adam have been forbidden from doing: eat the fruit from the tree of knowledge. When Adam and Eve refuse, having been warned by the angel Raphael to resist any further temptations on this score, Satan returns disguised as a snake. He tells Eve that God is simply jealous of them and does not want them to become as Gods too, which would surely happen once they ate the forbidden apple. Eve finally gives way, and is then joined by Adam, determined now to share her fate. Adam and Eve are expelled from paradise, and in due course must die as the direct result of their one, great sin.

Pullman first came across *Paradise Lost* at the age of sixteen when he studied its first two books at school. Immediately swept away by the majesty of the language and the power of the poetry, he also found it a superb story. In an interview years later he quotes the following lines that he still knows by heart:

> High on a throne of royal state, which far
> Outshone the wealth of Ormus and of Ind,
> Or where the gorgeous East with richest hand
> Showers on her kings barbaric pearl and gold,
> Satan exalted sat, by merit raised
> To that bad eminence.
>
> (*Paradise Lost*, Book II, lines 1–5)

For Pullman, this not only conjures up a vivid and compelling picture; it also raises the questions: 'What's

15. 'High on a throne of royal state, which far / Outshone the wealth of Ormus and of Ind, / Or where the gorgeous East with richest hand / Showers on her kings barbaric pearl and gold, / Satan exalted sat' (II, 1–5). (Source: *Doré's Illustrations for "Paradise Lost"*, Gustave Doré. Copyright © 1993 by Dover Publications, Inc.)

going to happen next? What's he going to do?' So while he went on to reject the theological argument about the Fall of Man on which the poem is based, he was happy to draw much of his inspiration from it. Such borrowings include the phrase *His Dark Materials*, the overall title for his trilogy, which comes from the poem and is quoted just before the first page of *Northern Lights*. It refers to the mixture of water, earth, air and fire involved in the creation of the world and now at large in the wild shores of Hell.

The overlap between *Paradise Lost* and Pullman's trilogy is not exact. While Lord Asriel shares some of Satan's malign energy, he is also an individual in his own right whose life path in the trilogy is never predictable. Nor is Lyra a direct replica of Eve.

In *Paradise Lost*, Milton wrote of Adam and Eve after they have been expelled from paradise:

> The world was all before them, where to choose
> Their place of rest, and Providence their guide;
> They hand in hand with wandering steps and slow
> Through Eden took their solitary way.

This is a sad image of two lost souls uncertain where to go next. But in Pullman's re-working of this great poem, Will and Lyra now have the entire world before them as well as their own spirits still intact and ready for the next challenge. The contrast could hardly be greater.

But what the two works do have in common, other than the basic Christian framework from which they make such different deductions, is a richness of imagination. Milton's brooding landscapes are echoed throughout Pullman's work, and there is also a common cast of angels, good and bad. Most importantly, both writers offer readers a trip into an imaginative world where wonders literally never cease but whose central core is still primarily about the eternal struggle between good and evil.

William Blake

Another of Pullman's heroes is the poet and artist William Blake, born in London in 1757. Blake believed that it is in the freedom of the imagination rather than in rational thought that we can best perceive the nature of the divine love and sympathy which surrounds us all. As he wrote himself, 'If the doors of perception were cleansed everything would appear as it is, infinite' (*A Vision of the Last Judgement*). Only after that can humans hope to discover 'the real and eternal world of which the Vegetable Universe is but a faint shadow.' (*Jerusalem*)

Blake was also much taken with the contrast between innocence and experience, writing his most famous sequence of poems around this theme. Several are about a 'Little Girl Lost' whose name is

Lyca, a possible inspiration for the Lyra of *His Dark Materials*. The tension between innocence and experience is also a preoccupation with Pullman, who sees advantages in both states, with experience the natural replacement of innocence rather than its inevitable corruption. Blake also believed that the human soul must first pass through the fallen world before it can reach a new, higher state of innocence. This idea is an obvious influence in those scenes in *The Amber Spyglass* where Lyra and Will visit the underworld and then emerge as newly purified beings.

Blake wrote in his principal prose work, *The Marriage of Heaven and Hell*, that the ultimate aim of all humans should be to enter the New Jerusalem of the redeemed imagination. For him, this involves the denial of eternal punishment and ultimate authority – views that have strong connections to Pullman's thinking as well. In *Milton*, one of his last works, Blake portrays the great poet returning from eternity in order to correct his former views about Original Sin. He now preaches a doctrine of self-sacrifice and forgiveness and denounces what he has come to see as the evil committed by God.

The principal enemies of the individual when it comes to making the spiritual journey through the fallen world from darkness to light are what Blake described as the various spectres that haunt us and which we must always learn to cast away. For Blake, such spectres are the creation of oppressive religion backed up by the state. His views are summed up in lines like 'God and his priest and King, / Who make up a heaven of our misery' (*Songs of Innocence and Experience*). Pullman too describes the equally dangerous and destructive Spectres in his stories as symbolic, in the way that they suck out an individual's soul, of the type of depression that can render any human life temporarily unbearable.

As part of his denial of the existence of the material world and nothing else, Blake insisted that at times he talked regularly to angels. Pullman also uses angels in his trilogy, along with other mythological or fabulous creatures. This is not because he too believes in the everyday existence of such things. But as regularly re-occurring symbols within the human imagination over the centuries, he clearly thinks that they must by definition stand for something important to all of us. Bringing them into play in a modern story helps build a bridge between today's readers and the most popular fantasies of the past, with the final effect of underlining the continuity of the whole of the human imagination over the centuries.

Heinrich von Kleist

The third major literary influence upon Pullman, Heinrich von Kleist, was born in 1777 and became an army officer before taking up philosophy. But after reading the works of the great German philosopher Immanuel Kant, Kleist came to the conclusion that human beings would always be incapable of arriving at the absolute truth about anything. Abandoning philosophy in order to become an author, he wrote several plays and many short stories. Eventually sinking into despair, he shot himself in 1811 as part of a suicide pact made with a woman suffering from incurable cancer.

His essay *On the Marionette Theatre* was written a year before his death, and is reprinted at the end of this book. Working from the observation that marionettes being set to dance always seem less affected than any human performers, Kleist describes how all individuals, following the example first set by Adam and Eve, have at some stage to become self-conscious. This means that everyone has to lose the child-like spontaneity and grace found in their younger years. The only way to re-enter this former paradise of total lack of self-consciousness is by working through the experience that accompanies adulthood, including those lessons learned through suffering, sorrow and other personal difficulties. So while it may be sad to lose the sort of innocence that marked us out as children, this is no tragedy. Instead, we can use our adult knowledge to recreate the same type of grace again, once we have discovered enough about ourselves and others to acquire the type of wisdom all humans are capable of through hard work and a life lived to the full.

There are obvious connections with *His Dark Materials* here, not least the mention in Kleist's essay of an Iorek-type tethered fighting bear who still manages to get the better of a nobleman armed with a sword and skilled in fencing. Like Kleist, Pullman also sees the story of Adam and Eve as symbolising the way that children have eventually to grow up by eating from the tree of knowledge. But this inevitable step forward should always be seen as an important acquisition rather than as any sort of dreadful loss or crime. This is because the loss of innocence also marks the beginning of wisdom.

Lyra and Will too have to sacrifice their innocent but sadly impractical desire to spend the rest of their lives together, while Lyra also loses her unconscious ability to work the alethiometer. But by fully engaging with the life in front of her, she will one day learn how to use the alethiometer again, but this time through hard work rather than through any innate skill. Or as Kleist puts it, 'we must eat again of the tree of knowledge a second time in order to return to the state of innocence.' This particular state is best symbolised by those older characters in *His Dark Materials*, such as Farder Coram, John Faa and Lee Scoresby, whose sound and selfless advice to Lyra is always worth listening to. This is not simply because they have already seen and learned so much during their long lives; it is also because they have reached a level of moral wisdom that only experience linked to self-knowledge can truly bring about.

Pullman, C.S. Lewis and growing up

Although Pullman is on record for despising the Christian-based Narnia stories of C.S. Lewis, the two writers actually share a good deal of background. Both lost a parent when young and later spent most of their adult life in Oxford. Both are fascinated by ideas of Northernness, and both create worlds separate from this one where children are put to severe moral tests before finally saving both themselves and everyone else. These tests include withstanding guilt about a sick mother left behind but still in desperate need of a cure. In Lewis's *The Magician's Nephew*, the child Digory is tempted to break a solemn promise by the hope that he might be able to help his sick mother. In *The Subtle Knife*, Will almost gives way when he has a vision of his own mentally ill mother's suffering face just as he is about to wield the knife that will finally cut the world free. Each writer also describes mighty battles within which the good finally manage to defeat the bad.

The Narnia stories famously start with a child

161

making a voyage to another land that exists at the back of a wardrobe. In the opening pages of *Northern Lights*, Lyra too hides inside a wardrobe, shutting the door just as the much-feared Steward, who has twice beaten her before, enters the room where she is not supposed to be. This surface similarity between the two stories comes up again at other points. The pitiless Tartars that kidnap Lyra, for example, are reminiscent of the Calormenes in Lewis's *The Last Battle*, with 'their white eyes flashing dreadfully in their brown faces.' Pullman may at other times be deliberately imitating the Narnia stories in order then to highlight the fundamental differences that exist between Lewis's approach and his own.

As Pullman has said himself, he had long 'wanted to give a sort of historical answer to the, so to speak, propaganda on behalf of religion that you get in, for example, C.S. Lewis.' But by attacking Christianity through its own story of the Garden of Eden, Pullman also succeeds in giving at least this part of the Bible an increased visibility that may otherwise have been lost on generations of younger readers. At a time when Bible stories are becoming less common in a great many schools, some young readers could now find themselves learning about some of the great stories of Christianity from Pullman himself. If this is an irony, Pullman would surely take it in good heart. Brought up on Bible stories as a child, he has never wavered in his love for them purely as stories. It is when they become dogma that he and they part company.

While Lewis follows the orthodox Christian values of his time, Pullman breaks away from them in anger and disgust. In Lewis's *The Last Battle*, one of the main child characters, Susan, is accused by another of the same age of being 'interested in nothing nowadays except nylons and lipstick and invitations. She always was a jolly sight too keen on being grown-up.' Pullman, on the other hand, welcomes and celebrates the onset of sexuality and the way this changes the relationship between Will and Lyra. In one beautiful passage, Lyra listens to Mary Malone, now taking on the role of serpent in the Garden of Eden. This is because, by talking about an old love affair, she gradually causes Lyra to feel herself coming alive in a new and passionate manner by way of response.

> She felt a stirring at the roots of her hair: she found herself breathing faster. She had never been on a roller-coaster, or anything like one, but if she had, she would have recognized the sensations in her breast: they were exciting and frightening at the same time, and she had not the slightest idea why. The sensation continued, and deepened, and changed, as more parts of her body found themselves affected too. She felt as if she had been handed the key to a great house she hadn't known was there; a house that was somehow

inside her, and as she turned the key, deep in the darkness of the building she felt other doors opening too, and lights coming on.

This lyrical description is reminiscent of the joy felt for each other by Adam and Eve in Book 4 of *Paradise Lost*. They too experienced sexual feelings without any of the attendant guilt that afflicted them later on after they had eaten the apple and then realised, for the first time, that they were both naked and ashamed. But Lyra is presented here as an Eve who is never going to experience the equivalent of the Fall, since the Church authorities that would once have imposed shame upon her are now a spent force. Will, when he reciprocates these feelings, also feels nothing but tenderness and love. What a pity, Pullman seems to be saying here, that the sexual instinct has not always been celebrated in this way rather than reviled in the spirit of religiously based disgust.

In Pullman's trilogy, Will and Lyra end their story determined to live their lives in the here and now. They have already discovered that the best way to survive the afterlife is to take with them as many positive stories about their former life as possible, of the type that are enjoyed at the time and then remembered with pleasure and affection afterwards. But the essence of all these stories must be their truthfulness, even if this means sometimes recalling painful as well as pleasurable moments and events from the past.

Even more importantly, they have just fallen in love and exchanged first, passionate embraces. This moment occurs just after Lyra offers Will some of the sweet-tasting red fruit packed for them by Mary Malone that morning. The symbolism is clear: Eve once again is offering fruit to Adam, but now that the Church and Christianity has finally been sent packing there is no one else around to tell them that what feels so good is wicked and bad.

Except, however, for the lone assassin Father Gomez, who for a few moments has Lyra in the telescopic sites of his powerful rifle and is about to pull the trigger. But he is eliminated at the last moment by Balthamos, one of the good angels, just as Eve was once given support by those angels still fighting against the tyranny of Heaven. In the Bible story, Eve lost; in this one, she wins. And at the same moment, 'The Dust pouring down from the stars had found a living home again, and these children-no-longer-children, saturated with love, were the cause of it all'. The victory of the new Adam and Eve is therefore complete. Humanity itself, having previously taken the false path of shame and guilt, can now follow in the same direction as Will and Lyra, unhampered by the past and full of hope for the future.

In the final book of the Narnia series, *The Last Battle*, the children discover that the land they are in is actually heaven. Without realising it, they have all been killed in a railway accident, but find that they are now so happy and fulfilled that they no longer miss any of their former times on earth. But Pullman takes a totally different view in his novels. For him, life on earth is the best there is ever going to be. The contrast could hardly be greater.

The occasional overlaps that do exist between Lewis and Pullman arise for a variety of reasons. Both are authors with a strong sense of mission. Their sense of a world divided between good and evil, and the way that all individuals have to take sides in this eternal battle, actually have a lot in common. Where they differ is over the whole question of Christianity. But at other times, particularly when the forces of light are battling it out with the powers of darkness, they become far more alike. At these moments, neither writer has much time for moral ambiguity in their books. Always happy to fight the good fight, both have little patience with waverers and the faint-hearted. Readers who have previously enjoyed the Narnia stories might therefore find much in *His Dark Materials* that could seem pleasantly familiar as well as deeply enjoyable in its own right.

Pullman's Philosophy

In the lecture given on the whole topic of the republic of Heaven already referred to, Pullman quotes G.K. Chesterton's remark that once people stop accepting organised religion they will in future believe not so much in nothing but in anything. There are moments in the trilogy when Pullman too seems attracted to alternative belief structures, such as the I Ching form of reading the future originating from China. But at base *His Dark Materials* is a strongly humanist text, celebrating the abiding existence of human courage and essential goodness.

Pullman has said that we can remain true to ourselves and to everyone else by constantly renewing our human faith not by religious belief but with the aid of those stories that remind us of the best we should aspire to. For Pullman, 'They are easily the most important things in the world. Within them we can find the most memorable, life-enhancing glimpses of human beings at their very best.' These are the same types of stories that the ghosts and harpies in *The Amber Spyglass* need in order to renew hope in their place of suffering.

But everyone needs good stories, not just ghosts. In his lecture, quoted above, Pullman writes that 'A republic that's only believed because it *makes more sense* or it's *more reasonable* than the alternative would be a pallid place indeed, and it wouldn't last for long. What induces that leap of commitment is an emotional thing – a story.' And by writing a best-seller that has given pleasure and consolation to many thousands of readers of all ages and nationalities, Pullman has provided such a story himself.

But if it is human folly and greed that is responsible for what Pullman sees as the crippling religious myths that he attacks in his trilogy, what force or forces produce the ghouls, cliff-ghasts and various other apparitions that appear throughout his story? There is no answer to this question, just as there is no explanation in his books for the existence throughout history of closed, evil minds over and beyond anything that could possibly be attributed to the malign influence of organised Christianity.

It would be mistaken to blame Pullman for this. He is writing a story, not a work of philosophy or history. His own strong views form an important part of what he writes, but it is as a work of fiction that these novels should be assessed. If there are inconsistencies in his judgements or gaps in his arguments, these only matter if belief in the story itself also becomes stretched as a result. To date, there are no signs that this has ever been the case with his multitude of readers, young and old.

Nor is Pullman interested in working out a complete cosmology for the largely imaginary worlds he is describing. Unlike the sagas of J.R.R. Tolkien, there are no accompanying maps in *His Dark Materials*. Nor are there any notes on the language, history and geography of the different people and objects of the type included by Tolkien in *The Lord of the Rings*. Although Pullman shares Tolkien's belief in the huge importance of story in the human imagination, he has no wish to treat his own particular tales as if they were truly describing something real.

Yet as an experienced storyteller, used to entertaining first his own brother as a child and then the various pupils he later taught in schools, Pullman also knows that outsize villains help make good tales. Most of the supernatural nasties in his books simply exist in their own right without any reason or explanation. Readers are unlikely to object, since it is these same evil forces that give the trilogy some of its most memorable moments.

So while the reason for the persistence of evil in human affairs is only partially explained in the trilogy, it does seem clear that dæmons play a large part where individual health and happiness are concerned.

When Spectres suck out these dæmons, or when the dæmons themselves have been cut away from their owners, individuals become mere shadows of themselves. They are also open to every bad influence that might now come their way unopposed.

Dæmons therefore have much in common with the religious concept of the soul, particularly in those cases where the dæmon is internalised and can't therefore be seen. It is always potentially at risk simply because it is so precious, and must be carefully tended and listened to at all times. Will comes to the conclusion, for example, that his mother's madness was caused by invisible Spectres trying to get a grip on her own dæmon, spirit, soul or whatever other word is used to stand for the moral core of a human being. To lose a soul, or to live with a corrupted one, as Mrs Coulter does with her golden-monkey dæmon, is to live in a spiritual desert. Those like the legendary Dr Faust or the apprentice Karl in Pullman's story *Clockwork*, who both make a pact with the devil involving the selling of their own soul, are as doomed as any of the dæmonless zombies found in Pullman's fiction.

As for the Spectres, old Giacomo Paradisi tells Will and Lyra that they 'are our fault, our fault alone. They came because my predecessors, alchemists, philosophers, men of learning, were making an enquiry into the deepest nature of things. They became curious about the bonds that held the smallest particles of matter together … We undid them, and we let the Spectres in'. He adds that where the Spectres actually came from remains a mystery, but 'what matters is that they are here, and they have destroyed us.'

This makes Spectres symbolic of what can go wrong when humankind meddles with matters that should be left alone. An equivalent destructive curiosity found in our own world might arguably include the sort of scientific enquiry that led to the development of nuclear weapons and, later on, to controlled genetic mutations. But there is another possible explanation for Spectres which reaches into the psychological rather than into history or politics. The description of what happened to Lena the witch after a Spectre invades her body is also like reading about a bad attack of depression.

> She felt a nausea of the soul, a hideous and sickening despair, a melancholy weariness so profound that she was going to die of it. Her last conscious thought was disgust at life: her senses had lied to her; the world was not made of energy and delight but of foulness, betrayal, and lassitude. Living was hateful and death was no better, and from end to end of the universe, this was the first and last and only truth.

On this reading, assault by the Spectres brings about the feelings of ultimate despair that also become a possibility every time an individual decides to open a window into a parallel world, purely of his or her own imagination, and then attempts to take up residence there. However glorious the initial prospects and however friendly its inhabitants, those who go on to live too long in their own imaginative world eventually risk alienation or even madness. Once the real world comes to seem a poor, uninviting place by comparison, the incentive to return to it may increasingly diminish. Those who want to make the return journey may also discover that the beings in this imaginary world are not always as benign as they might first appear.

The classic description of this process is found in Joanne Greenberg's magnificent autobiographical novel, *I Never Promised You a Rose Garden*. The mentally ill narrator, with the help of a sensitive psychotherapist, finally tries to leave the fantasy world she has been content to live in for the real one instead. She then discovers that the imaginary friends who once meant so much to her now turn into pitiless tormentors, anxious to prevent her return to reality – and therefore her cure – at all costs. As a believer in the necessity for living to the full in the world as we know it, Pullman might be hinting here that Spectres do indeed stand for the type of depressive illness that can strike against the very will to live itself. As a metaphor, this is as good as any for describing the process whereby an individual suffering from depression sometimes seems to lose touch altogether with the essential, inner spirit necessary for their personality to function normally.

The best fantasy writing has always meant quite different things to different readers, so there can never be a definitive answer as to what exactly Spectres, or indeed any other characters in Pullman's work, are intended to symbolise. Stories like his that have the power to stimulate strong, imaginative reactions in different readers, even though these reactions may differ radically from one person to another, are sometimes described as 'mythopoeic'. This defines writing that is powerful enough to create its own myths and in doing so give shape to readers' various fears and fantasies. On this basis alone, Pullman's trilogy is an outstanding achievement. In an age in search of new myths to replace some of the older ones from former years, *His Dark Materials* is a text that has already talked directly to thousands of readers. It provides not just entertainment but also extra meaning to many readers and to their own most personal fantasies.

Is there a paradox in the way that Pullman, an anti-Christian, uses Christian symbolism throughout his writing? Angels both good and bad, Adam and Eve, prophecy and the idea of destiny, images of pilgrimage, the importance of the soul and the notion of heaven and hell all play vital parts in his narrative. Milton and Blake, both widely quoted, were Christian writers, and there are also quotations from the Bible and Christian poets such as George Herbert and Andrew Marvell.

But although the architecture and symbolism in *His Dark Materials* largely derive from Christian sources, the emphasis is mostly on how it all went wrong. In this sense, the trilogy is not so much an atheist text as a reworking of a Christian one towards radically different conclusions. As an intensely moral writer, Pullman seems naturally drawn towards Biblical imagery of good and evil of the type that has played such a key part in the history of the Western world.

Yet as a humanist and freethinker, he hates the guilt and repression that, in his view, also lie at the basis of Christianity. The end result is a story that sets out not so much to demolish the value of the religious impulse experienced by so many human beings but to push it in a totally different direction. Believing that there is more to life than simple materialism, he creates instead an alternative vision of the world that shares a Christian notion of a divine presence some-where and somehow, but rejects all the definitions and claimed manifestations of it of the type recorded in the Bible.

Fundamentalist Christians reject the theory of

evolution, preferring to believe that God himself created all known species. Evolutionists take an opposite line, convinced that Darwin's theory of natural selection shows how species can change without any need of divine intervention. Pullman too belongs to this particular camp, but adds that now humans are on the scene there is also the chance to direct all future development rather than simply wait passively for more evolutionary change.

All the living beings on earth found in *His Dark Materials* are the result of evolution. One example of this is demonstrated to Mary Malone when she learns about the ways that the mulefa have developed over the centuries through constant interaction with the seed-pods that are so important to them. Pullman himself has described the process of human evolution as blind and automatic, and accepts the Darwinian notion of natural selection as the only acceptable explanation for how it all works. But because humans have consciousness, he also believes that this potentially alters the future processes of evolution. As he says in his lecture on the republic of Heaven, 'We might have arrived by a series of accidents, but from now on we have to take charge of our fate. Now we are here, now we are conscious, we make a difference. Our presence changes everything.'

In *His Dark Materials*, Will and Lyra show how two people can have a profound effect upon the future as well as the present. But their victory is hard won rather than inevitable, and if some of the evil characters had prevailed instead, the outcome would have been disastrous. So although Pullman believes that human beings can make all the difference in the way that their own species continues to adapt to the world, he also makes it clear that such change always has the potential to be either good or bad.

Conclusion

At the moment when Will and Lyra shyly handle each other's dæmons for the first time, they cease to be children. From this time forward, their dæmons will take on a permanent shape, and Will and Lyra will move towards that adult state which, throughout the trilogy, was always shown as naturally attracting more Dust than was the case with childhood. Dust, mislabelled by Christianity and the Church as Original Sin, clearly stands in this context for a state of heightened self-consciousness, linked in this case to a first experience of sexual delight. How far Lyra and Will actually go down this road is deliberately left unclear, with Pullman himself admitting that 'They have their moment of bliss – whatever it is (and I don't know what it is).' But given their tender ages, any first expression of physical love – even a passionate embrace – has the capacity to come over as an event of such mind-blowing proportions that ordinary life may indeed never seem the same afterwards.

The end of childish innocence that accompanies

first sexual consciousness is also associated with the beginning of adult wisdom. So although Lyra can no longer read her alethiometer, having lost the particular state of innocent grace that once enabled her to do so, she can still recover this skill through hard work. As the Angel Xaphania puts it to her, 'Your reading will be even better then, after a lifetime of thought and effort, because it will come from conscious understanding. Grace attained like that is deeper and fuller than grace that comes freely, and furthermore, once you've gained it, it will never leave you.'

This, then, is the journey that the first Eve also had to take after she ate the apple that symbolised sexual and intellectual awareness. Lyra has to make it too, but now she is unpunished by those ecclesiastical forces that vilified the first Eve and have done their level best to eliminate the second one. She can therefore come into her adulthood without shame, showing her fellow humans an altogether better way to live and in so doing destroy the negative powers of the Church for ever. This she achieves when her own new-found state of happiness and fulfilment goes on to fill the rest of the world with the same vivid sense of loving awareness, while she and Will 'lay together as the earth turned slowly and the moon and stars blazed above them.'

By leading the suffering ghosts from the underworld of the dead, Lyra also puts right one last great wrong that occurred when Adam and Eve were expelled from the Garden of Eden. Previously immortal, they were then told of the certainty one day of their own death. But liberating the ghosts, by allowing them back into a world where they can now happily disappear, replaces the Christian notion of death with the idea of a natural re-absorption into the atmosphere. Any idea of eternal punishment in hell or reward in heaven is therefore dropped in favour once again of another type of immortality. For although all ghosts disappear once they leave the underworld, they will still always be present in an invisible world where they are now at one and at peace with everything else. Lord Asriel's original prophecy in *Northern Lights*, that death itself was going to die, therefore finally comes about, although he had not known at the time that it was his daughter who was going to deliver this essential freedom rather than himself.

By making Will and Lyra – like Romeo and Juliet – separate just as they have finally found each other, Pullman also ensures that this first vision of young love remains for ever unsullied by any of the practical difficulties or inevitable disagreements that creep into even the most ideal of human relationships. It would, in fact, have been difficult to imagine these two characters from different worlds living happily together in either one or the other place for the rest of their lives. Both children also have a lot of growing up to do, with neither of their worlds looking particularly kindly upon a passionate love affair between two people so young. But as the last and most powerful symbol in the trilogy, love at its first and most intense still serves Pullman's overall message well. It makes an unforgettable case for the way that humans can, and should, always seek to discover and realise the state of heaven that lies within and between themselves rather than forever looking for it elsewhere.

Even so, some have found this final separation something of an anti-climax. Will and Lyra resolving to spend the rest of their lives properly in their separate worlds is admirable in itself, but hardly measures up against the enormity of their loss. When the angel Xaphania tells them how to set about living a good life, she sounds more like an old-fashioned schoolmistress than a divine presence. As she puts it, Lyra and Will can preserve the precious Dust now flowing back into the world by helping others 'to learn and understand about themselves and each other and the way everything works, and by showing them how to be kind instead of cruel, and patient instead of hasty, and cheerful instead of surly, and above all how to keep their minds open and free and curious.'

It is also implicit in Pullman's writing that Will and Lyra have it within them to overcome their loss by determining to give their all to the life they have remaining to them. Only then will they be able to play their part in building the republic of heaven which, to a certain extent, must always rely upon those concerned giving up some of what they most want in order to benefit everyone else. Had either Will or Lyra insisted on the other going with them to their world, this act of putting their own needs first would have made it impossible for them then to live the sort of life they were hoping for. It would also have deprived readers of an ending that remains extremely moving because it is also so sad.

So the whole idea of going off with each other, rather than staying in their old worlds, represents a final temptation for Will and Lyra to put their own good above everything else. The first Eve fell for the temptation of acquiring true knowledge and under-standing, and again Pullman thinks she was right to do so. Lyra, the second Eve, resists the temptation of selfishness, and this time Pullman is on her side. For a true republic of heaven needs people who 'have to be all those difficult things like cheerful and kind and curious and brave and patient, and we've got to study and think, and work hard, all of us, in all our different worlds'. Backing up this fairly demanding summons, Pullman quotes in his lecture on the republic of Heaven the nineteenth-century writer George Eliot's comment after talking about God, Immortality and

16. The botanic gardens, Oxford. At the end of *The Amber Spyglass*, Will and Lyra agree to go to the same bench in these gardens in their separate worlds – at midday on Midsummer's Day every year for as long as they live.

Duty; 'How inconceivable the first, how unbelievable the second and yet how peremptory and absolute the third.'

As Pullman adds himself, 'I like this earnestness. I admire it a great deal.' Yet he feels something to be lacking here, which for him is the accompanying sense of joy that he also believes is a natural, as well as necessary, part of living. Even so, it is perhaps ironic that a trilogy written against Christianity should end on this note of self-denial. The angel's message urging Lyra and Will towards making an even greater effort in their future lives would not have been out of place in those many improving children's books from the past that regularly used to carry a Christian message as well.

Pullman is a strongly idealistic writer, naturally drawn to other thinkers and authors before him who have also striven to find morals and meanings in the universe. At a time when Christianity was the universal belief, it is inevitable that these voices were mostly Christian at base, whatever their occasional surface disagreements with organised religion. But in a modern Western world where the orthodox Christian story looks increasingly remote and unbelievable, Pullman provides readers with a different type of spiritual journey.

His Dark Materials is written in a religious framework in the sense that it also searches for an ultimate meaning to the age-old problem facing all readers of why exactly they are here and what they should then be doing about it. Yet while Christianity sought answers to this question in the theology Pullman so dislikes, he meets this challenge through the imagination. For it is in stories, and the way they can renew faith both in ourselves and in others, that he has always chosen to operate, and never more effectively than in this particular trilogy. Its large sales suggest that in an increasingly Godless age the appetite still remains for literature that powerfully engages readers with its own type of spiritual quest.

Uniquely for a book written for children, *The Amber Spyglass* won the Whitbread Award in 2001 for the best book of the year. It was also long-listed for the Booker Prize – another award normally going to novels written with only an adult audience in mind. Having once produced school plays that entertained both parents and pupils, Pullman has now achieved the same aim with these books. This success was particularly gratifying for him, given that he has always believed that the best children's literature has universal appeal. As he said in his acceptance speech when winning the Carnegie Medal in 1995 for *Northern Lights*, 'Only in children's literature is the story taken seriously.'

In the same vein, he has stated elsewhere that 'Children's books still deal with the huge themes which have always been part of literature – love, loyalty, the place of religion and science in life, what it really means to be human. Contemporary adult fiction is too small and sterile for what I'm trying to do.' The great success of his trilogy suggests that the desire among all ages for novels which take up these big themes is as strong as ever.

So too is there a universal need for convincing fantasy where the good finally prosper and the bad come to a sorry end. In real life it is often hard to tell which the good side is and even harder to assess whether it truly does come off better at the finish. A story that raises such questions and then comprehensively answers them clearly has a lot going for it. But no book ever survives on the merits of its ideas alone. *His Dark Materials* is also beautifully written in language that is clear, direct and easy on the ear. There is no tired English in this saga, just as there are no over-familiar plot devices. The windy rhetoric found in some other fantasy sagas is avoided in favour of short sentences that always manage to say exactly what they mean, even when there is something complex to get across.

Pullman has himself spoken about how best to write in a lecture delivered in New York in April 2002:

> The aim must always be clarity. It's tempting to feel that if a passage of writing is obscure, it must be very deep. But if the water is murky, the bottom might be only an inch below the surface – you just can't tell. It's much better to write in such a way that the readers can see all the way down; but that's not the end of it, because you then have to provide interesting things down there for them to look at. Telling a story involves thinking of some interesting events, putting them in the best order to bring out the connections between them, and telling about them as clearly as we can.

To read these books aloud, as Pullman has done in an audio version, is to experience at first hand how easily they flow and how well each character is caught. If the many younger readers who have enjoyed these books also pick up some of Pullman's limpid prose style at the same time, they will be learning from someone who is a master not just of the imagination but also of written English. Equally at home both with everyday dialogue and with those moments when his imagination soars to meet the challenge of describing scenes of great, sometimes unearthly, beauty, he has never written better or to greater effect. His trilogy, with its extraordinary power and unforgettable impact, represents the culmination of a long apprenticeship in writing, starting off the day after he left university and finally climaxing in one of the most ambitious and far-reaching works of imagination ever to appear in either children's or adult fiction.

Bibliography

Bibliography

Books by Philip Pullman

Galatea, London: Gollancz, 1978; New York: Dutton, 1979

Count Karlstein, or the Ride of the Demon Huntsman, London: Chatto and Windus, 1982

Count Karlstein, or the Ride of the Demon Huntsman, graphic-novel version illustrated by Patrice Aggs, London: Doubleday, 1991

Count Karlstein, or the Ride of the Demon Huntsman, with a new introduction, London: Doubleday, 2002

The Ruby in the Smoke, Oxford: Oxford University Press, 1985

How To Be Cool, London: Heinemann, 1987

The Shadow in the North, Oxford: Oxford University Press, 1987

Spring-Heeled Jack; a Story of Bravery and Evil, London: Transworld, 1989

The Broken Bridge, London: Macmillan, 1990

The Tiger in the Well, Harmondsworth: Penguin, 1992

The White Mercedes (*The Butterfly Tattoo*), London: Macmillan, 1992

The Tin Princess, London: Penguin, 1994

Thunderbolt's Waxwork, London: Viking, 1994

The Firework-Maker's Daughter, London: Doubleday, 1995

The Gas-Fitters' Ball, London: Penguin, 1995

Northern Lights (*His Dark Materials: Book One*), London: Scholastic, 1995. Published with the title *The Golden Compass* in the USA, New York: Knopf, 1996

Clockwork, or All Wound Up, London: Doubleday, 1996

The Subtle Knife (*His Dark Materials: Book Two*), London: Scholastic, 1997

Mossycoat, London: Scholastic, 1998

I Was a Rat, or The Scarlet Slippers, London: Doubleday, 1999

The Amber Spyglass (*His Dark Materials: Book Three*), London: Scholastic, 2000

Puss in Boots, London: Doubleday, 2000

Plays

Frankenstein, adaptation of the novel by Mary Shelley, Oxford: Oxford University Press, 1990

Sherlock Holmes and the Adventure of the Limehouse Horror, London: Nelson, 1993

Secondary Sources

Annotations for Philip Pullman's *His Dark Materials* trilogy, Robot Wisdom website: www.robotwisdom. com/jorn/darkmaterials.html

Bird, Anne-Marie, 2000, 'Dust, Dæmons and Soul States: Reading Philip Pullman's "His Dark Materials"', *BALC Bulletin*, number 7, ISSN: 1363-1764

Bird, Anne-Marie, 2001, 'Without Contraries is no Progression. Dust as an all-inclusive multifunctional metaphor in Philip Pullman's "His Dark Materials"', *Children's Literature in Education*, Vol. 32, no. 2

Brown, T., 2000, interview with Philip Pullman, Amaranth website: www.avnet.co.uk/home/ amaranth/Critic/ivpullman.htm

Eccleshare, J., 1996, 'Northern Lights and Christmas Miracles', *Books for Keeps*, 100:15

Fox, G., 1997, 'Authograph 102: Philip Pullman', *Books for Keeps*, 102

Gevers, N., 2000, 'Philip Pullman: *The Subtle Knife*', review on *infinity plus* website: www.iplus.zetnet. co.uk/nonfiction/subtle.htm

Lenz, Millicent, 'Philip Pullman', in *Alternative Worlds in Fantasy Fiction*, edited by Peter Hunt and Millicent Lenz, London: Continuum, 2001

Lenz, Millicent, 2003, 'Story as a Bridge to Transformation: The Way Beyond Death in Philip

Pullman's "The Amber Spyglass"', *Children's Literature in Education*, volume 34, number 1

Odean, K., 2002, 'The Story Master', 6 October article, School Library Journal website: www.slj.com/articles/articles/20001001_9064.asp

Pullman, P., 1998, 'Let's Write it in Red: the Patrick Hardy Lecture', *Signal 185*

Pullman, P., 1996, excerpt from Carnegie Medal Acceptance Speech, Random House Kids website: www.randomhouse.com/features/goldencompass/subtleknife/speech/html

Pullman, P., 2000, 'Achuka Interview: Philip Pullman', Achuka Children's Books website: www.achuka.co.uk/ppint.htm

Pullman, P., 'The Dark Side of Narnia', *Guardian*, 4 October 1998

Pullman, P., 'The Republic of Heaven', *Horn Book*, Vol. LXXV11, number 6, 2001

Pullman, P., 'Voluntary Service', *Guardian*, 28 December 2002

Pullman, P., 'Dreaming of Spires', *Guardian*, 27 February 2002

Pullman, P., *One Way Home*, part of a series of conversations with authors and psychoanalysts, London: Institute of Psychoanalysis, 2003

Spanner, Huw, 2000, Interview with Philip Pullman, Third Way website: www.thirdway.org.uk/past/showpage.asp?page=3949

Tucker, Nicholas, 'Paradise Lost and Freedom Won', interview in the *Independent*, 28 October 2001

Vincent, Sally, 'Driven by Emotions', interview in the *Guardian*, 10 November 2001

Appendix

On the Marionette Theatre

by Heinrich von Kleist
Translated by Idris Parry

One evening in the winter of 1801 I met an old friend in a public park. He had recently been appointed principal dancer at the local theatre and was enjoying immense popularity with the audiences. I told him I had been surprised to see him more than once at the marionette theatre which had been put up in the market-place to entertain the public with dramatic burlesques interspersed with song and dance. He assured me that the mute gestures of these puppets gave him much satisfaction and told me bluntly that any dancer who wished to perfect his art could learn a lot from them.

From the way he said this I could see it wasn't something which had just come into his mind, so I sat down to question him more closely about his reasons for this remarkable assertion.

He asked me if I hadn't in fact found some of the dance movements of the puppets (and particularly of the smaller ones) very graceful. This I couldn't deny.

A group of four peasants dancing the rondo in quick time couldn't have been painted more delicately by Teniers.

I inquired about the mechanism of these figures. I wanted to know how it is possible, without having a maze of strings attached to one's fingers, to move the separate limbs and extremities in the rhythm of the dance. His answer was that I must not imagine each limb as being individually positioned and moved by the operator in the various phases of the dance. Each movement, he told me, has its centre of gravity; it is enough to control this within the puppet. The limbs, which are only pendulums, then follow mechanically of their own accord, without further help. He added that this movement is very simple. When the centre of gravity is moved in a straight line, the limbs describe curves. Often shaken in a purely haphazard way, the puppet falls into a kind of rhythmic movement which resembles dance.

This observation seemed to me to throw some light at last on the enjoyment he said he got from the marionette theatre, but I was far from guessing the inferences he would draw from it later.

I asked him if he thought the operator who controls these puppets should himself be a dancer or at least have some idea of beauty in the dance. He replied that if a job is technically easy it doesn't follow that it can be done entirely without sensitivity. The line the centre of gravity has to follow is indeed very simple, and in most cases, he believed, straight. When it is curved, the law of its curvature seems to be at the least of the first and at the most of the second order. Even in the latter case the line is only elliptical, a form of movement natural to the human body because of the joints, so this hardly demands any great skill from the operator. But, seen from another point of view, this line could be something very mysterious. It is nothing other than *the path taken by the soul of the dancer*. He doubted if this could be found unless the operator can transpose himself into the centre of gravity of the marionette. In other words, the operator *dances*.

I said the operator's part in the business had been represented to me as something which can be done entirely without feeling – rather like turning the handle of a barrel-organ.

'Not at all', he said. 'In fact, there's a subtle relationship between the movements of his fingers and the movements of the puppets attached to them, something like the relationship between numbers and their logarithms or between asymptote and hyperbola.' Yet he did believe this last trace of human volition could be removed from the marionettes and their dance transferred entirely to the realm of mechanical forces, even produced, as I had suggested, by turning a handle.

I told him I was astonished at the attention he was paying to this vulgar species of an art form. It wasn't just that he thought it capable of loftier development; he seemed to be working to this end himself.

He smiled. He said he was confident that, if he could get a craftsman to construct a marionette to the specifications he had in mind, he could perform a dance with it which neither he nor any other skilled dancer of his time, not even Madame Vestris herself, could equal.

'Have you heard', he asked, as I looked down in silence, 'of those artificial legs made by English crafts-men for people who have been unfortunate enough to lose their own limbs?'

I said I hadn't. I had never seen anything of this kind.

'I'm sorry to hear that', he said, 'because when I tell you these people dance with them, I'm almost afraid you won't believe me. What am I saying ... dance? The range of their movements is in fact limited, but those they can perform they execute with a certainty and ease and grace which must astound the thoughtful observer.'

I said with a laugh that of course he had now found his man. The craftsman who could make such remarkable limbs could surely build a complete marionette for him, to his specifications.

'And what', I asked, as he was looking down in some

perplexity, 'are the requirements you think of presenting to the ingenuity of this man?'

'Nothing that isn't to be found in these puppets we see here,' he replied: 'proportion, flexibility, lightness ... but all to a higher degree. And especially a more natural arrangement of the centres of gravity.'

'And what is the advantage your puppets would have over living dancers?'

'The advantage? First of all a negative one, my friend: it would never be guilty of affectation. For affectation is seen, as you know, when the soul, or moving force, appears at some point other than the centre of gravity of the movement. Because the operator controls with his wire or thread only this centre, the attached limbs are just what they should be ... lifeless, pure pendulums, governed only by the law of gravity. This is an excellent quality. You'll look for it in vain in most of our dancers.'

'Just look at that girl who dances Daphne', he went on. 'Pursued by Apollo, she turns to look at him. At this moment her soul seams to be in the small of her back. As she bends she looks as if she's going to break, like a naiad after the school of Bernini. Or take that young fellow who dances Paris when he's standing among the three goddesses and offering the apple to Venus. His soul is in fact located (and it's a frightful thing to see) in his elbow.'

'Misconceptions like this are unavoidable,' he said,

'now that we've eaten of the tree of knowledge. But Paradise is locked and bolted, and the cherubim stands behind us. We have to go on and make the journey round the world to see if it is perhaps open somewhere at the back.'

This made me laugh. Certainly, I thought, the human spirit can't be in error when it is non-existent. I could see he had more to say, so I begged him to go on.

'In addition', he said, 'these puppets have the advantage of being for all practical purposes weight-less. They are not afflicted with the inertia of matter, the property most resistant to dance. The force which raises them into the air is greater than the one which draws them to the ground. What would our good Miss G. give to be sixty pounds lighter or to have a weight of this size as a counterbalance when she is performing her entrechats and pirouettes? Puppets need the ground only to glance against lightly, like elves, and through this momentary check to renew the swing of their limbs. We humans must have it to rest on, to recover from the effort of the dance. This moment of rest is clearly no part of the dance. The best we can do is make it as inconspicuous as possible.'

My reply was that, no matter how cleverly he might present his paradoxes, he would never make me believe a mechanical puppet can be more graceful than a living human body. He countered this by saying that, where grace is concerned, it is impossible for man to come anywhere near a puppet. Only a god can equal inanimate matter in this respect. This is the point where the two ends of the circular world meet.

I was absolutely astonished. I didn't know what to say to such extraordinary assertions.

It seemed, he said as he took a pinch of snuff, that I hadn't read the third chapter of the book of Genesis with sufficient attention. If a man wasn't familiar with that initial period of all human development, it would be difficult to have a fruitful discussion with him about later developments and even more difficult to talk about the ultimate situation.

I told him I was well aware how consciousness can disturb natural grace. A young acquaintance of mine had as it were lost his innocence before my very eyes, and all because of a chance remark. He had never found his way back to that Paradise of innocence, in spite of all conceivable efforts. 'But what inferences', I added, 'can you draw from that?'

He asked me what incident I had in mind.

'About three years ago', I said, 'I was at the baths with a young man who was then remarkably graceful. He was about fifteen, and only faintly could one see the first traces of vanity, a product of the favours shown him by women. It happened that we had recently seen in Paris the figure of the boy pulling a thorn out of his foot. The cast of the statue is well known; you see it in most German collections. My friend looked into a tall mirror just as he was lifting his foot to a stool to dry it, and he was reminded of the statue. He smiled and told me of his discovery. As a matter of fact, I'd noticed it too, at the same moment, but ... I don't know if it was to test the quality of his apparent grace or to provide a salutary counter to his vanity ... I laughed and said he must be imagining things. He blushed. He lifted his foot a second time, to show me, but the effort was a failure, as anybody could have foreseen. He tried it again a third time, a fourth time, he must have lifted his foot ten times, but it was in vain. He was quite unable to reproduce the same movement. What am I saying? The movements he made were so comical that I was hard put to it not to laugh.

'From that day, from that very moment, an extra-ordinary change came over this boy. He began to spend whole days before the mirror. His attractions slipped away from him, one after the other. An invisible and incomprehensible power seemed to settle like a steel net over the free play of his gestures. A year later nothing remained of the lovely grace which had given pleasure to all who looked at him. I can tell you of a man, still alive, who was a witness to this strange and unfortunate event. He can confirm it, word for word, just as I've described it.'

'In this connection', said my friend warmly, 'I must tell you another story. You'll easily see how it fits in here. When I was on my way to Russia I spent some time on the estate of a Baltic nobleman whose sons had a passion for fencing. The elder in particular, who had just come down from the university, thought he was a bit of an expert. One morning, when I was in his room, he offered me a rapier. I accepted his challenge but, as it turned out, I had the better of him. It made him angry, and this increased his confusion. Nearly every thrust I made found its mark. At last his rapier flew into the corner of the room. As he picked it up he said, half in anger and half in jest, that he had met his master but that there is a master for everyone and everything – and now he proposed to lead me to mine. The brothers laughed loudly at this and shouted: 'Come on, down to the shed!' They took me by the hand and led me outside to make the acquaintance of a bear which their father was rearing on the farm.

'I was astounded to see the bear standing upright on his hind legs, his back against the post to which he was chained, his right paw raised ready for battle. He looked me straight in the eye. This was his fighting posture. I wasn't sure if I was dreaming, seeing such an opponent. They urged me to attack. 'See if you can hit him!' they shouted. As I had now recovered somewhat from my astonishment I fell on him with my rapier. The bear made a slight movement with his paw and parried my thrust. I feinted, to deceive him. The bear did not move. I attacked again, this time with all the skill I could muster. I know I would certainly have thrust my way through to a human breast, but the bear made a slight movement with his paw and parried my thrust. By now I was almost in the same state as the elder brother had been: the bear's utter seriousness robbed me of my composure. Thrusts and feints followed thick and fast, the sweat poured off me, but in vain. It wasn't merely that he parried my thrusts like the finest fencer in the world; when I feinted to deceive him he made no move at all. No human fencer could equal his perception in this respect. He stood upright, his paw raised ready for battle, his eye fixed on mine as if he could read my soul there, and when my thrusts were not meant seriously he did not move. Do you believe this story?'

'Absolutely', I said with joyful approval. 'I'd believe it from a stranger, it's so probable. Why shouldn't I believe it from you?'

'Now, my excellent friend,' said my companion, 'you are in possession of all you need to follow my argument. We see that in the organic world, as thought grows dimmer and weaker, grace emerges more brilliantly and decisively. But just as a section drawn through two lines suddenly reappears on the other side after passing through infinity, or as the image in a concave mirror turns up again right in front of us after dwindling into the distance, so grace itself returns when knowledge has as it were gone through an infinity. Grace appears most purely in that human form which either has no consciousness or an infinite consciousness. That is, in the puppet or in the god.'

'Does that mean', I said in some bewilderment, 'we must eat again of the tree of knowledge in order to return to the state of innocence?'

'Of course,' he said, 'but that's the final chapter in the history of the world.'

1810

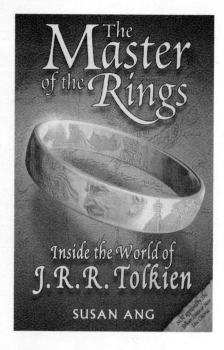

The Master of the Rings: Inside the World of J.R.R. Tolkien

Susan Ang

J.R.R. Tolkien is the greatest fantasy writer ever to have lived. He has millions of devoted readers worldwide, and over 100 million copies of his books have been sold. And now he has a new legion of fans, thanks to the film versions of *The Lord of the Rings.*

The Master of the Rings takes a look at the man himself, where he came from, what influenced his writing, and the themes that unite his major works, *The Hobbit* and *The Lord of the Rings*. There's also a detailed guide to who's who, what's what and where's where in Middle-earth, and a unique look at the historical background to *The Lord of the Rings*. This is the perfect companion to Tolkien's stories.

UK £5.99 • Canada $12.00 • ISBN 1 84046 423 2

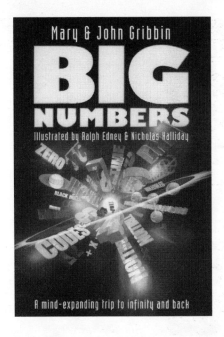

Big Numbers: A mind-expanding trip to infinity and back

Mary and John Gribbin
Illustrated by
Ralph Edney and
Nicholas Halliday

How big is infinity? How small is an electron?
When will the Sun destroy the Earth?
How fast is a nerve impulse in your brain?
Why can't you see inside a black hole?
What's the hottest temperature ever recorded on Earth?
What's the furthest you can see on a clear night?

Welcome to the amazing world of 'Big Numbers', where you'll travel from the furthest reaches of the known Universe to the tiniest particles that make up life on Earth. Together with Mary and John Gribbin, you can find out how our telescopes can see 10 billion years into the past, and why a thimble-full of a neutron star would contain as much mass as all the people on Earth put together!

UK £6.99 • Canada $15.00 • ISBN 1 84046 431 3

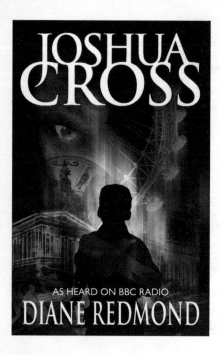

Joshua Cross

Diane Redmond

It is only when a monstrous centaur appears from nowhere to chase him along the Thames Embankment that Joshua Cross becomes aware of his destiny.

Swept back in time to Ancient Greece, Josh begins an epic journey that will lead him to the very depths of the Underworld. But before he can return home, Josh must face the man who destroyed his father, and who wants to kill *him*, alone.

UK £4.99 • Canada $12.00 • Paperback • ISBN 1 84046 466 6

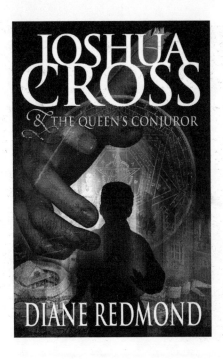

Joshua Cross and the Queen's Conjuror

Diane Redmond

Joshua Cross's enemy, Leirtod, is back with a vengeance ...

Swept back to 1590s London and placed in the care of Dr Dee, the Queen's Conjuror – a mathematician, astrologer, and occasional dabbler in the occult – Joshua soon discovers that he's in mortal danger. With his so-called protector intent on finding the elixir of life – no matter what the cost – and his friend Dido bound up in the court of Queen Elizabeth, Josh's future looks increasingly perilous.

This is an action-packed novel that treads the dark side of the Elizabethan court where treachery and intrigue abound.

UK £10.00 • Canada $20.00 • Hardback • ISBN 1 84046 487 9
Published April 2004

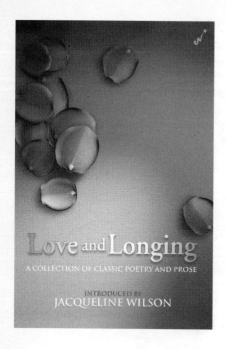

Love and Longing: A collection of classic poetry and prose

Introduced by Jacqueline Wilson
Edited by Kate Agnew

Wizard is proud to introduce a collection of classic poetry and prose extracts based around the enduring themes of love and romance, with an introduction by prize-winning children's author **Jacqueline Wilson**.

From the intensity of a first love through the pleasures of persuasion and passion, to the pain of parting, *Love and Longing* is a collection of classic love poetry and prose that explores this enduring theme's many facets.

Contents

Includes poems by Elizabeth Barrett Browning, Tennyson, Shakespeare, Charlotte Mew, Robert Herrick, Aphra Behn, Catullus and Donne as well as extracts from *Jane Eyre*, *North and South*, *Wuthering Heights* and other writings.

All royalties from this book will go to the charity National Children's Homes.

* * *

Jacqueline Wilson is one of Britain's best-loved children's authors and has sold over 10 million books in the UK alone, winning countless awards in the process. Four of her books made the BBC's recent Big Read Top 100 and she is the most borrowed children's author in the country's libraries. In June 2002 Jacqueline was given an OBE for services to literacy in schools.

UK £ 4.99 • ISBN 1 84046 523 9 • Published 5 February 2004

Fear and Trembling:
A collection of classic poetry and prose

Introduced by Kevin Crossley-Holland
Edited by Kate Agnew

Wizard is proud to introduce a collection of classic poetry
and prose extracts based around the intriguing themes of
horror, haunting and the macabre, with an introduction by
prize-winning children's author **Kevin Crossley-Holland**.

The sinister, the macabre, and the gory have long exerted
a powerful hold on the imagination. *Fear and Trembling*
contains poems and prose extracts with a heady mix of the
supernatural, horror, suspense, gothic and the spine-tingling
that will have you on the edge of your seat.

Contents

Includes poems by Shelley, Edgar Allen Poe, Oscar Wilde, James Macpherson, Browning, Blake, Thomas Gray and Mary Robinson as well as extracts from *Beowulf*, *Doctor Faustus*, *The Yellow Wallpaper*, *Frankenstein* and the Bible.

All royalties from this book will go to the charity National Children's Homes.

* * *

Kevin Crossley-Holland is a highly regarded poet, story-teller and Fellow of the Royal Society of Literature. His acclaimed book, *Arthur, the Seeing Stone*, won the *Guardian* Children's Fiction Award and was shortlisted for the Whitbread Award and the Smarties Prize. The third part of his best-selling trilogy, *King of the Middle March*, is out this Autumn.

UK £ 4.99 • ISBN 1 84046 526 3 • Published 5 February 2004